THE
ONE-SHOT
LIBRARY
INSTRUCTION

THE ONE-SHOT LIBRARY INSTRUCTION

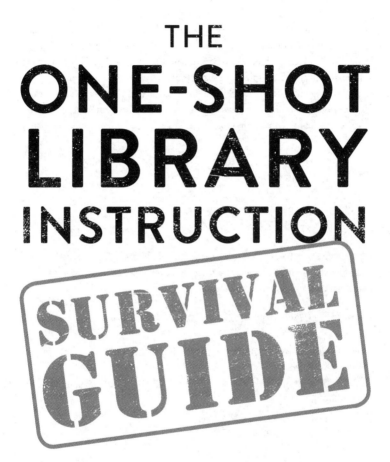

HEIDI E. BUCHANAN & BETH A. McDONOUGH

An imprint of the American Library Association

Chicago | 2014

Heidi Buchanan and **Beth McDonough** have more than thirty years combined experience teaching information literacy. An MSLS graduate of the University of North Carolina–Chapel Hill and head of research and instruction services at Western Carolina University, Buchanan is a graduate of the ACRL's Information Literacy Immersion program and is certified as a master trainer by the State Library of North Carolina. McDonough holds an MLIS from the University of North Carolina–Greensboro, and is completing a dissertation about critical information literacy for an EdD in leadership of curriculum and instruction from Western Carolina University. She is a National Board certified teacher in school library media, and currently works as a research and instruction librarian at Western Carolina University.

© 2014 by the American Library Association

Printed in the United States of America
18 17 16 15 14   5 4 3 2 1

Extensive effort has gone into ensuring the reliability of the information in this book; however, the publisher makes no warranty, express or implied, with respect to the material contained herein.

ISBN: 978-0-8389-1215-7 (paper).

Library of Congress Cataloging-in-Publication Data
Buchanan, Heidi E.
  The one-shot library instruction survival guide / Heidi E. Buchanan and Beth McDonough.
        pages   cm
  Includes bibliographical references and index.
  ISBN 978-0-8389-1215-7 (alk. paper)
  1. Library orientation for college students. 2. Information literacy—Study and teaching (Higher) 3. Research—Methodology—Study and teaching (Higher) 4. Academic libraries—Relations with faculty and curriculum. I. McDonough, Beth. II. Title.
  Z711.25.C65B83 2014
  025.5'677—dc23

                                                                    2013044168

Cover design by Kim Thornton.
Text design by Kirstin Krutsch in the Brandon Grotesque Bold, Midiet Serif, and Arno Pro typefaces.

⊚ This paper meets the requirements of ANSI/NISO Z39.48-1992 (Permanence of Paper).

CONTENTS

"They Never Told Me This in Library School"

This book is inspired by the thousands of librarians across the country who regularly teach one-shot library instruction. We were surprised several years ago when our Association of College and Research Libraries (ACRL) workshop about one-shot library instruction quickly filled to capacity with sixty-two librarians eager to learn new teaching strategies, with even more on the waiting list. It turns out that though many librarians want to be excellent teachers, they encounter significant barriers to their success, including the need for collaboration with course instructors, the pressure to cover proliferating information literacy objectives in a limited amount of time, the desire to engage students successfully, and the need to assess the success (or failure) of their teaching session. It doesn't help that most teaching librarians were not offered any formal preparation to teach in their graduate programs. The stories we heard that day, and in subsequent workshops, became the outline for the chapters of this book. Despite the barriers, most teaching librarians earnestly want to help their students become information-literate, and most understand that they must change their teaching practices if that is to happen. This book will invite you to turn your everyday challenges into instruction that is meaningful and relevant for your students. Not only can it be done, but you can do it.

Reaching a common understanding of information literacy is problematic, not just with course instructors, but even within our own profession. The literature is flooded with articles that endlessly debate the concept of information literacy and the best way to deliver it. Surprisingly, one-shot library instruction receives less attention, though it continues to be the most common form of library instruction. Embedded librarianship, interactive online tutorials, and credit-bearing information literacy courses are all well and good, but of little use to the librarian who has one-shot library instruction as a major job responsibility and is faced—sometimes on a daily basis—with teaching a diverse range of students in multiple disciplines how to transform a vast amount of information into academic scholarship.

What Is the One-Shot?

Instead of serving as the instructor of record for an entire course, librarians often work with a class for a single session, generally only 50 to 75 minutes in length. These single sessions are commonly referred to among teaching librarians as "one-shots." Critics of one-shot instruction object to the generic library orientation or tour, which fits more into the traditional category of bibliographic instruction rather than information literacy instruction. Even in 2012, when reporting data for the ACRL, librarians are asked to record the number of "presentations" instead of "classes." One-shot library instruction does not have to be a dog-and-pony show about library resources or locations. Instead, as with any library instruction, it should teach students to find, evaluate, and use information when faced with an information need. It is not a library tour, orientation, scavenger hunt, or an isolated session that isn't tied to a course or part of an academic curriculum. The premise of information literacy is that the individual must "need" the information, so it is important that any one-shot library session be based on that need.

It is quite possible that your one-shot library instruction may not have made the transition to true information literacy instruction as described above. Even after two decades of professional focus on the concept of information literacy, many librarians are still practicing bibliographic instruction. Seamans (2012) describes this phenomenon as "a tendency to take bibliographic instruction, wave a wand over it, and designate it as information literacy instruction" (230–31). She borrowed Ward's (1997) chart to answer the question, "How Is Information Literacy Different from Bibliographic Instruction?" (231). Examine table 1.1 and ask yourself: "Which column most accurately reflects my instruction practices?" If the answer is that you are still a bibliographic instructor, don't be dismayed. The solutions offered in this book will help you to transform your instruction in the desired direction.

TABLE 1.1

HOW IS INFORMATION LITERACY DIFFERENT FROM BIBLIOGRAPHIC INSTRUCTION? (WARD 1997, AS CITED IN SEAMANS 2012)

Bibliographic Instruction	Information Literacy
1. One-shot instruction	Integrated into curriculum
2. Focuses on learning to use library resources	Focuses on information management
3. Often not linked to classroom assignments	Integral to course assignments
4. Session often focuses on passive learning	Active learning
5. May lack clearly defined goals and objectives	Goals and objectives are carefully linked to course
6. Librarian lectures, demonstrates	Librarian and faculty facilitate learning
7. Librarian provides instruction asked for	Librarian and faculty design and implement together

Why Bother?

One major challenge that all librarians have is the issue of time. Librarians have many other responsibilities in addition to teaching, so the idea of investing additional time into planning and implementing one-shot sessions may seem counterintuitive. Why invest quality time in your one-shots? The most obvious reason is that if you only get one session with a group of students, you want to teach it well and make it relevant and meaningful. Another reason is that your investment in collaboration with the course instructor will develop into a positive working relationship and lead to future endeavors, such as a more integrated model of information literacy instruction. The time you spend reflecting on your teaching after a class session is a valuable investment as well. The more time you spend preparing for and reflecting upon a class, the less stress you will have in the classroom.

If you are looking for a cookbook of ready-made lesson plans or a linear template for your instruction, this is not the book for you. A premise of this book is that meaningful, relevant information literacy instruction begins with the student experience. Since every student or group of students is different, every instructional situation is different as well. Librarians' situations also vary widely. Have you ever read an article or heard a conference presentation and thought, "that's nice, but it would never work in my library"? There are no cookie-cutter solutions. You will want to adapt the recommendations in this book to your "real life" and choose the strategies that work best for your own teaching. It is also understood that there are many things that you cannot control, such as institutional frameworks, resources, or technology; but there are many more that you can control, and those are the focus of this book. If you concentrate on those areas that you can control, your instruction will improve, and chances are you will feel better about yourself as a teacher. In fact, it may just become your favorite part of your job.

Despite these disclaimers, this book offers invaluable guidance based on decades of classroom experience, wisdom from the literature, and voices from the field. We wrote the book that we wish we had read our first year of teaching. The fact that you have purchased this book attests to your willingness and readiness to improve your instructional practices, so turn the page and begin to become a better, more confident teacher.

"The Teaching Faculty Won't/Don't _____"
Communicating and Collaborating with Instructors

If you only read one chapter in this book, let this be it. In a nutshell, your success as a teaching librarian rests squarely on your ability to communicate and collaborate effectively with course instructors. This chapter will help you to develop these professional relationships and set the stage for partnership. It also includes examples of opening lines for conversation, suggestions for the negotiation process, or instruction interview, and classroom-tested ideas for planning a one-shot session designed around specific learning goals and the course research assignment(s). Finally, this chapter offers an important time saver for every teaching-librarian—when (and how) to say no!

Communication and Collaboration with Course Instructors

Building sustainable relationships with course instructors is critical to your success and one of the hardest aspects of the job. The emphasis on partnership in the one-shot instruction model is important for very practical reasons:

- Clear communication and conversation with the course instructor will help you design your class session; you will need to know where the students are and what they are expected to do (see chapter 3).
- The success of one-shot instruction depends on the course instructor to reinforce information literacy, in class and through their assignments. Recent studies including the ERIAL Project and Project Information Literacy (Duke and Asher, 2012; Head and Eisenberg, 2009) suggest that students typically ask their instructor for research help first, and it is the instructor who often guides the student back to the library.
- The partnership that begins with a one-shot session is the building block for integrating instruction more completely into the course curriculum (see chapter 7).

Strong collaboration takes time and is often a gradual, trust-building process. By its nature, collaboration can also be frustrating, uncomfortable, and time-consuming. So why bother? If course instructors and librarians do not communicate and collaborate successfully, "the student becomes the frustrated loser" (Feldman and Sciammarella 2000, 495). Also, collaboration often results in better products and instructional outcomes than can be produced in isolation (Brown and Duke 2006).

Significant barriers to communication and collaboration exist. Most of these barriers are due to misperceptions—from both librarians and course instructors. Whereas librarians might feel that course instructors are possessive of their time, curriculum, and students, course instructors may feel pressure by the amount of content they need to teach and are loath to give up scarce instructional time. Many course instructors are not aware of all of the library services that are available, or they worry that they are asking too much of the librarian. As with many misperceptions, there are elements of truth to these feelings, but librarians and faculty can work together to clear up the misperceptions. There are many success stories; much of the literature indicates that faculty are open to collaboration with librarians. After all, course instructors and librarians have more similarities than differences—most importantly a common concern about student success. If you keep student learning front and center, collaboration will naturally follow. Focus on similarities and don't make assumptions about what course instructors won't do.

Set the Stage for Collaboration

There are many different approaches to collaboration and communication with course instructors. Styles vary widely based on the personalities of the collaborative partners. As with many aspects of teaching librarianship, collaborative skills are often learned through trial and error. Here are some general guidelines, which you can adapt to varying situations.

Be Visible (and Pay Attention)

Librarians work in a misunderstood profession. For better or worse, the librarian of public opinion is a keeper of books (and sometimes cardigans and cats). Course instructors rarely think of librarians as teachers, even though more than half of all academic librarian jobs require some teaching (Albrecht and Baron, 2002; Clyde, 2005). Unfortunately, course instructors do not spend much time thinking about faculty-librarian partnerships at all, so it is up to librarians to capture their attention. Course instructors need and *want* clear communication from librarians about the kinds of instructional services they offer. As one professor put it, "I think [the library] is an underutilized resource and probably largely because people don't know all the things that can be done . . . I think more outreach is necessary" (Armstrong 2012, 42–43).

Certainly library outreach, marketing, and public relations can help educate faculty about library resources and services, but if you don't have time to launch a full-scale campaign, don't worry. The easiest way to build awareness is to *demonstrate to your constituents what you really do*—displacing stereotypes with lived experiences.

One way to be visible is to reinforce your role as teacher—attend teaching workshops alongside the course instructors, participate in curriculum committees, and offer workshops for faculty that model your best pedagogical practice. Another way to stay visible is to take positive perceptions and use them to your advantage. However your teaching-faculty colleagues view you—as helper, researcher, collector, archivist, organizer, or protector of intellectual freedom—all roads lead to information literacy!

Even if you don't have the resources for a marketing campaign, you do have the resources to communicate what is available to course instructors. Tailor your communication to your audience. Choose your approach and timing wisely; for instance, when a course instructor complains about grading poorly researched papers, it is a perfect opportunity to offer a librarian intervention for the next semester. Often the best partnerships evolve from casual conversations, rather than flashy flyers, spam e-mail, or clever giveaways. Avoid inundating faculty with information and be sensitive to their perceived domain over their curriculum and ownership of their class time.

Pay attention! Remember that listening to the needs and interests of the course instructor is a necessary part of good communication. Ask them about the things that concern them: their students, their courses, their scholarship, departmental culture, and so on. Demonstrate your interest (and knowledge of information) in their disciplines. Send them a note acknowledging their latest publication; notify them of relevant new books and articles in their specific research areas. If you get faculty talking about their own reading, research, and writing, you can segue into conversations about their expectations for their students' reading, research, and writing. The process of listening also leads to a deeper collaboration; what Raspa and Ward call a "bond of belonging" (2000, 1).

Approach Course Instructors as Equals and Focus on Common Goals

Librarians are sensitive to issues of professional identity. This sensitivity may be compounded for academic librarians whose careers both parallel and are yet markedly different from teaching faculty (Walter, 2005). Teaching faculty and the general public have many misconceptions about librarians that feed this sensitivity. The good news is that such sensitivity is a state of mind and thus can be overcome. In your approach to teaching faculty as equal colleagues, it's important to focus on the many similarities and common goals that teaching librarians and teaching faculty share.

One similarity is that most librarians and teaching faculty in higher education did not go to school to be teachers. Most course instructors, outside of the discipline of education, have no more teaching preparation in their coursework than librarians do. The fact that both teaching faculty and teaching librarians are underprepared to teach may not sound like much cause for celebration, but this shared experience does lay the groundwork for an equal professional partnership that both parties can approach with confidence.

The key similarity that librarians and teaching faculty share is the common goal of student success. Course instructors do not want to grade bad research papers and projects. We all want students to be able to find, evaluate, use, and share information effectively and responsibly. With this in mind, guide your conversations with faculty toward what they want their students to be able to do. Be sure you are speaking the same language; course instructors probably won't be fluent in ACRL standards, but can articulate their expectations for their students. For example, their expectations might include: to develop better critical thinking skills, to use better sources, to solve specific problems, to understand the literature of the discipline, or to avoid plagiarism.

Teaching faculty and teaching librarians also share a comfort level and facility for academic research that their students may not have. Both sides of the teaching librarian/course instructor partnership can provide valuable insights about how students interact with information—this dialogue can lead to successful collaborations in information literacy instruction.

Form Relationships and Keep Talking

Relationships go deeper than contacts. Solid working relationships involve a "real conversation" about common goals (Gallegos and Wright 2000, 98). On the one-shot level, this real conversation includes developing goals together and reflecting together after the class. Instead of trying to collaborate with an entire department at once, focus on individual, professional connections and build from there. Don't underestimate the value of "the hallway conversation." The trick to turning hallway conversations into collaborative ventures lies in timely and appropriate follow-up by the librarian. It isn't quite as simple as, "Here's that book you mentioned, and by the way, how would you like to develop an assignment together?" but almost! Table 2.1 offers sample conversation starters.

The Instruction Interview

In the frenzy of a new semester it is easy just to book library sessions like you would a hotel room. Requests fly in at a rapid pace and you need to get them on your calendar. You ask the basic questions such as *How many students do you have? What will your class be working on?* Many libraries have online forms for the course instructor to fill out. The problem with booking the class session in this way is that it leaves little room for the "real conversation" this chapter encourages you to have with the course instructor. Planning the library session is just an information problem like any other, and good librarians already have the negotiation skills in place to solve it: the reference interview. Apply the same strategies of the reference interview to the instruction request process. At the reference desk, it takes some negotiation to establish what the student is actually asking for—the same applies to instruction.

TABLE 2.1

CONVERSATION STARTERS

Instead of: "Here's a copy of the ACRL standards, let me know how you plan to incorporate them . . ."	*Try: I see that your department's program goals include responsible information use and critical thinking; there are ways I can help you meet those goals.*
Instead of: Inwardly grumbling about Dr. So-and-so's research assignment . . .	*Try: I noticed at the reference desk that your students need to find [cases, company info, literary criticism, etc.]. Would you like me to teach a workshop for the whole class?*
Instead of: Waiting for the phone to ring . . .	*Try: What types of library research assignments will your students be working on this semester?* • *Would you like to schedule a library instruction session?* • *Would you like a series of library sessions? [bold]* • *When would you like to schedule a series of sessions? [bolder]* • *I'm coming to your class on January 3 [too bold!]*
Instead of: "You really need to schedule another library instruction session for that class . . ."	*Try: What kinds of instructional aids would work best for complementing the library session?* • *Online tutorial?* • *Research guide?* • *Office hours with a librarian later in the semester?* • *Follow-up sessions with the librarian?*
Instead of: "Sure, I'd be happy to give a library tour on your first day of class . . ."	*Try: Our classes work best when they reach students at the point of need. Let's wait until they've explored a bit, and then conduct a librarian intervention. At what stage of the research process do you think your students need the most help?*

Course instructors will ask for what they think you can provide, based on their own perceptions of what librarians do. You will need to negotiate with the instructor to identify and focus the intended learning goals, and establish the best ways to meet those needs. The teaching librarian's mantra should be to push back without being pushy. As one faculty member surveyed by Jeffries (2000) stated, "Be bold, but not too bold" (125). The Talking Points chart below provides some suggestions for the instruction interview.

In the tradition of the generic library tour, many course instructors want to schedule library instruction the first week or two of the semester, long before students will begin their research. This mismatch between the timing of the library session and the timing of the assignment results in library instruction that has little relevance for students. Faculty may assume that the teaching librarian can simply transfer a set of skills to the student to be recalled at will later in the semester, but of course the research process is much more complex than that. One professor commented in a recent e-mail responding to a draft of this chapter, "I think some of us expect miracles—taking reluctant or underprepared students from knowing nothing about research to polished scholarship in one session" (January 17, 2012). The instruction interview will help you and the professor identify the best time for the library session.

TALKING POINTS

What kinds of research will the students be doing? (Ask for a copy of the syllabus and research assignments.)

What does the course instructor expect the students to be able to do at the end of the session, and what is reasonable to expect after a 50- to 90-minute session? Be forthcoming about what can be accomplished in a one-shot session and work with faculty to focus the goals for the library instruction.

What stage of the research process will the students be in at the time of library instruction? When scheduling and planning a library instruction session, timing *really is* everything. For the same research assignment, your session could and should be noticeably different, depending on whether the students are in the beginning, middle, or end stages of their research——or, the worst of all, not yet begun (see "How (and When) to Say No" below). One of the most successful techniques is to try to push the timing of the library session to later in the semester so that you can provide just-in-time, student-centered instruction to support student learning when and where they need it. (See chapter 3 for more information about stages of research.)

Are they willing to assign "homework" before the session? This could be something simple like having the students bring in a resource that they have already found, or it could be more elaborate such as Bergmann and Sams's "flipped classroom" (2012) model described in chapter 7. Make sure you know whether the instructor wants you to grade this homework in any way——a graded homework assignment may motivate students to follow through.

Will follow-up sessions or supplementary instruction aids be needed? Many times course instructors will have unrealistic expectations of what can be accomplished in a single session. Don't hesitate to focus on the most important objectives, and offer to provide more research support through additional sessions or supplementary materials such as handouts or research guides. (See chapter 7 for more ideas.)

Tip: Just as you would in the reference interview, make summary statements to ensure that you have understood the request. For example, at the end of your conversation with the instructor: *So, I will plan on introducing [list a couple of basic concepts] for identifying and finding literary scholarship in Victorian British literature. You are going to send me a copy of the assignment this week, and I will call you in a few weeks to talk about my specific plan for the library session. Is this what you had in mind?*

The instruction interview should be a priority, even for last-minute requests. As you establish your working relationships with course instructors, this will happen more organically. As with the reference interview, you may need a series of instruction interviews to really make sure you and the course instructor are on the same page. Instructors will often want to take care of all of the planning before the semester begins and the class has even met, but it is important to have a follow-up conversation just before the session so you can both review your expectations for the class session, and tailor your class session to the actual needs of the students at that stage of the research process. The professor will have new information such as the class culture, which may affect the activities you choose for the class. The follow-up also gives you an opportunity to let the instructor in on your plans. Even during a very busy semester, this follow-up with the instructor is worth your time! It will help you avoid awkward scenarios such as the class showing up without knowing their assignment (or without their instructor). If the instructor knows your expectations and your plan, your session will go more smoothly. It also demonstrates preparation on your part—you don't have a canned instruction session that you teach to every class—and gives you credibility as a teacher.

LESSON LEARNED!

The forgotten art of face-to-face meetings or phone calls is most effective and efficient for the instruction interview. If you e-mail a list of questions, you may only receive an answer to the first one! As a general rule, any conversation that requires the exchange of three or more e-mails is an indication that a personal conversation is in order.

The Research Assignment

The research assignment should be fuel that drives the instruction interview. Set the tone of the conversation by finding something good to say about the assignment and asking questions. For example, a conversation starter such as, *I like it that you have built in time to talk with the students about their topics, early on . . . Do you find the conferences help-ful?* can lay the groundwork for a library session about how to refine a research topic.

While it's a good strategy to start the conversation with the assignment and the professor's ideas, you should be prepared with some ideas of your own. Involve the instructor in the planning of the library session. Explain your ideas and approach (as specifically as you feel necessary). Or, better yet, give the professor choices, and ask him or her to choose preferred strategies: *For this part of the library session, I would like the students to either work in small groups or two-person teams to brainstorm strategies. Which do you think will work best for this class?*

If there are serious problems with the assignment (for example, it refers students to resources that are not available in your library), you should point them out to the course instructor. How much input you offer will depend on your relationship, and whether there is reasonable time to make changes to the assignment. Many course instructors are open to cooperative design of research assignments. But, if time does not allow for revision of the assignment—and the problems don't stand in the way of student success—wait until after the session to offer input about the assignment for the next time.

How (and When) to Say No

Saying no does not come easily to many librarians because good librarians are helpers by nature. However, if you allow information literacy to be trivialized at your institution, you won't be helping anyone. It's okay to say no. If you want information literacy to be taken seriously, and librarians and course instructors to work *as equal partners/colleagues* toward the common goal of student success, there are times when saying no is the right thing to do. Muelemans and Carr (2013) agree that it is crucial for librarians to be clear with course instructors about their policies and expectations and to give honest input about things like class assignments: "The 'customer is always right' attitude is not an effective teaching or collaborative philosophy. This attitude will perpetuate an uneven relationship" (83).

Ideally, your program should have some instruction policies in place to support your no. Policies may be both written and unwritten. On paper, such a policy will require instructors to attend library sessions and *actively participate*. Course instructors should reinforce the importance of information literacy skills; and more practically, the course instructor needs to know what you did in class in order to point students back to those skills and resources as they progress on their projects. If your professor tells you that he or she cannot come to the session, firmly explain your policy and its rationale, and request that the session be rescheduled for a time when the professor can be there. If rescheduling isn't possible (*dire* emergencies only), ask that the class be accompanied by someone else from the department. Use this backup method sparingly, or you will encourage repeat offenders.

VIGNETTE: CLEAR COMMUNICATION (AND WHY TO SAY NO)
—*Kate Langan, Assistant Professor, Humanities Librarian, Western Michigan University*

The first semester that I started at Western Michigan University as the humanities librarian, I jumped in feet first and grabbed as many classes as possible. Most of them were integrated with the general education writing classes. Much to my surprise, the research assignments for these writing classes varied widely. I quickly realized that I needed to get detailed assignment information from the instructors in order to plan the sessions. However, I was wishy-washy and did not enforce my requests. Luckily, the majority of the classes went smoothly. I received the assignments and started to prep from there.

My approach quickly changed a few weeks into the semester. I was scheduled to teach a class on a Tuesday, but by Monday evening, I still had not heard from the instructor. I did not think twice about it. How bad could it be? It did not occur to me to say "No." On Tuesday morning, I met the students in the classroom. The instructor belatedly handed me two pages describing the assignment: to research the parts of an object and write a paper describing its history, tracing its fabrication from cradle to grave. I didn't even know where to begin.

I found myself in a classroom with ten students, varying objects in hand. Someone had a trophy; others had a baseball, a deck of cards, a plaque, a color photograph. The students had already written about their emotional connection to the object. Now they were to write an impartial, physical description of the piece. Without lead time, I completely misunderstood the assignment. It wasn't until twenty minutes into the class that I grasped the topic. I couldn't point them to useful information resources. It was a waste of time. I looked bad, and the students were bored.

I've since changed my approach to teaching in many ways. I will not teach without a copy of the assignment, syllabus, or a list of learning outcomes. The information literacy program is highly visible. In fact, it is a priority. The most important lesson I learned is that of communication. Every teaching librarian needs to communicate with faculty before teaching a class. But the conversation also needs to become department-wide. I became visible in the department, made contacts with coordinators and chairs. I started attending departmental meetings. When the English writing program was hiring a new coordinator, the English Department listened to my input. Now, when I ask for materials to assist in teaching, I get a quick response. Communication has allowed me to become an esteemed teaching resource for the department. With support from the faculty thanks to good communication, I have been able to develop stronger teaching assignments and know when to say "No." Everybody wins.

Avoid "milk and spinach"[1] sessions. In other words, if the instructor wants to bring the class to the library because it is good for them, but doesn't have a research assignment or other curricular tie-in, politely decline. Even library tours for first-year study skills classes should be connected to specific course-related learning goals. If students don't see an immediate and practical application to the library session, they won't be engaged and will quickly become indifferent to the idea of information literacy instruction.

Sometimes you have to be bold. Despite the care you put into the instruction interview and follow-up conversations, there will still be instructors who manage to elude you. If it is a few days before the library session and you still haven't received the necessary information about the assignment, then contact the faculty member to reschedule or cancel.

Summary

Communication and collaboration with course instructors are the cornerstones of successful information literacy instruction—and an important investment of your time. Course instructors and teaching librarians share the common goal of student success. Librarians can help clear up misconceptions and misunderstandings about information literacy and librarians as teachers by displacing stereotypes with lived experience: (1) be visible and pay attention, (2) approach faculty as equals and focus on common goals, and (3) form relationships and keep talking.

Negotiating library instruction sessions with teaching faculty requires similar skills as the familiar reference interview. It is an information problem that librarians can solve through guided questioning aimed at uncovering intended learning goals and the best way to achieve them.

The research assignment provides the basis for the instruction interview. While librarians have much to offer in terms of assignment design, and course instructors are typically open to working with librarians, your ability to influence the assignment might be limited by your relationship with the professor and the timing of the instruction interview during the semester. It is important to be able to push, but not be pushy.

Sometimes, you have to say no to preserve the integrity of your information literacy program. In such cases it is helpful to have written policies in place. Some policies may also be unwritten, but just good common sense. Library instruction that is conducted for its own sake and not tied to clear learning goals is often a waste of time—for you, the students, and the course instructor.

Note

1. The authors have heard this phrase used by librarians in informal settings, but the origins are unknown.

"But, How Will I *Cover* Everything?"

The impossibility of covering the material in a one-shot session is an oft-heard lament from teaching librarians. The concern is a valid one, but you can't possibly cover everything, so quit trying! You will have to step back and think about what you want the students to learn, and why—and then consider what is reasonable to expect from a one-shot session. This chapter will distinguish between teaching and covering, prompt you to start with the basics, help you let go of some well-intentioned but ineffective practices; and present a framework for designing library instruction that is useful and relevant to students at their points of need.

It's no wonder that teaching librarians often feel overwhelmed trying to teach information literacy via one-shot instruction sessions. The challenge is vast. The five standards outlined in the *Information Literacy Competency Standards for Higher Education* encompass 22 performance indicators, and 87 outcomes (ACRL, 2000). Similarly, *Standards for the 21st Century Learner* (AASL, 2007) encompasses 83 outcomes grouped into four categories!

"But how will I *cover* everything?" The truth is you won't, and attempting to do so guarantees frustration. Students become information-literate through supported practice over a long period of time, not as a result of one-shot library instruction. By its very nature, one-shot instruction is limited. Accepting that you aren't going to be able to *cover* all of the important information literacy skills established by the standards is the first step toward designing relevant, meaningful one-shot sessions.

So, what's the solution? Start by freeing yourself of the idea that you can transfer knowledge to students as if they were blank slates. When you try to cover everything you *tell* them what they need to know. So, if later they do not use the information skills, it's not your fault, right? After all, you told them the right way to do it. If only it were that easy.

Your challenge is not to cover the material, but rather to *teach* it. To teach well you need a fundamental understanding of constructivist learning theory. Constructivism frames learning as an active process in which the learner builds meaning by connecting new information to prior knowledge—"each higher, more complex, more sophisticated level of knowledge must be connected to, constructed from, a pre-existing foundation of knowledge" and thus cannot be simply transferred from teacher to student (Smilkstein 2006, 154). The difficult truth is that it really doesn't matter what you cover in the classroom; the student is only going to take away what he or she can put to effective use. The question becomes not "How will I cover everything?" but instead "What will the students take away that will be relevant and useful?"

Start with the Basics

Since you can't cover everything, the best strategy is to teach a few useful, relevant things well. With so many standards and objectives to address and no time to teach, take a critical look at your approach to library instruction and be prepared to let go of some of your current practices. Teaching librarians are not alone in facing the challenge of an overwhelming number of educational objectives. The "stuffed curriculum" is a challenge faced in many educational disciplines, particularly those that are rapidly changing (Cousin 2006, 4). Before you decide how to teach the class, consider what to teach, and more importantly, why you want to teach it.

Step back and think about your purpose for the class. Ask yourself: *What is most important for the students to take away from this class?* This question will help you get to the real heart of what you want to teach; your answer will help you define what Hilda Taba (1962) called the "fundamental rationale" (211). The answer to the takeaway question will likely not be a list of resources, but rather a few simple concepts or skills. Instead of demonstrating resources, focus on why you want to teach those resources, and most importantly, what students need to know for the resource to make sense.

Other disciplines have approached the problem of the stuffed curriculum by focusing on "threshold concepts," which Meyer and Land define as: "opening up a new and previously inaccessible way of thinking about something" (2006, 3). Townsend, Brunetti, and Hofer assert that "this [threshold concept] approach offers a way to focus and prioritize instructional content and leads to engaged teaching" (2011, 854). In other words, before teaching anything else, librarians often need to back up a little and look for the places where students get stuck. Hofer, Townsend, and Brunetti (2012) surveyed librarians and identified the following common "stumbling blocks" in information literacy instruction. A few are discussed below.

Web Search Engines vs. Databases

Students do not understand the differences between Web search engines and databases. They also commonly refer to Google or JSTOR as a source rather than a finding aid. When using databases, students first need to know what it is that they are searching—and how it differs from using other search engines or databases. Librarians often present databases and search engines as being similar, which can create unrealistic expectations for the process of searching and for the results of a search. Hofer, Townsend, and Brunetti (2012) discourage librarians from skipping over the "mechanics of a database." They advise librarians to introduce students to the more complex features that distinguish databases from Web search engines such as advanced searching and controlled vocabulary—all of which give students a bigger picture of the inner workings of a database as well as a hint that the research process may be more difficult than a simple Google search. Of course, the mechanics should only be introduced after students understand what they are searching for, *why* they are searching for it, and why that information might be in a database. Many of the nuts and bolts can be saved for a research guide or a tutorial.

Formats

The idea that the intellectual value of an information source is dependent on whether it is online or in print is a hole that librarians and instructors dug for themselves in the early online days. How many times have you offered students the perfect content for the project at hand, only to have them turn it down because of professor-proscribed limitations on format? These format limitations often contribute to student misunderstanding of information. For example, a student forbidden to use websites may not understand that the instructor may accept an e-book as a source. Respondents to the threshold concepts survey pointed out another common problem: "students tend to see all information as one amorphous mass rather than as specific sources produced by specific communities . . . differentiating formats is more difficult when we encounter everything online" (Hofer, Townsend, and Brunetti 2012, 398). Search engines, databases, and discovery services have made finding and searching easier in a lot of ways, but have made the format concept more challenging for students to grasp and librarians to teach. Hofer, Townsend, and Brunetti recommend that librarians emphasize "format as a process," that is, the difference in various sources "has nothing to do with how one accesses it . . . but with the process that went into creating it" (403).

Authority

Librarians and course instructors are also concerned that students struggle with evaluating sources and passively accept all sources as being of equal value. Students tend to put information in two categories, good or bad, when information rarely falls neatly into either category. For instance, a newspaper article may be considered a relevant and reliable source for one class project, but not for another. And not all newspapers are of equal quality and none are purely objective. Hofer, Townsend, and Brunetti state that "once students understand that authority doesn't just exist, but is constructed—and what constitutes authority changes depending on the context—they begin to understand that true objectivity is unattainable and authority is not monolithic" (403). This concept can be tough to teach and goes way beyond any sort of checklist you can give to students. Ultimately, they are forced to use their own judgment based on the context and the information they can gather. You may need to spend some time in class helping students establish a context for their information needs.

These stumbling blocks will not come as a surprise to any librarian who has been practicing for more than a week, but are a good reminder of important (and universal) concepts that are implicit to librarians' work and not so obvious to students. These hang-ups must be addressed before you launch into teaching other processes and details. Threshold concepts, when made explicit to students, present fertile ground for relevant, useful library instruction. Ask yourself if there are basic misunderstandings that once clarified can be transferred from one information problem to another. Focus on the basic understandings and skills that students need to be successful.

Ditch the Demo

There are a number of challenges for teaching librarians when it comes to designing relevant, useful instruction. In the one-shot environment, you are likely to have a range of students with varying levels of information-seeking ability and knowledge of library resources and services. The trick is to meet the students at their points of need, but the points of need can be challenging to identify. The safe and therefore tempting thing to do is to show the generic processes of searching for information, so that all students know how to do the bare minimum, such as search the library catalog and appropriate databases. Lessons become very tool-focused and core concepts can be overlooked. The trap is when you end up doing the same old things in every session—you know the drill—introduce a tool, demonstrate it, set aside a time for hands-on practice. As addressed in chapter 4, the notion that presenting a lecture and leaving some time at the end for hands-on practice equals active learning may be well intentioned, but is often ineffective. In essence, when teaching librarians use the demo approach they simply ask the student to mimic sequential processes, which falls far short of an authentic learning experience. Worse yet, establishing this pattern with your teaching practically guarantees that not only will the students be disengaged, but you will quickly become bored as well. If you are teaching the same thing the same way again and again, chances are you are not enjoying yourself, and it shows. Of course some demonstration of resources is often necessary, but keep it brief, and time it for when it will be meaningful for the students.

VIGNETTE: LETTING GO OF THE "SALES DEMO"
—*Jason Sokoloff, Business Librarian, James Madison University*

As the new business librarian, I inherited an instruction session for the gateway business class. All business undergraduates are required to take the gateway class in their junior year. The classes are large with up to eighty students in each section. The pivotal assignment is a business-plan project, where students work in groups of five or six to develop a simulated business plan.

The previous business librarian's instructional plan for this class involved two sessions each semester: an early introduction to fundamental business sources; and another near the middle of the term to review specialized topics and advanced searching techniques. At first I did not make any significant changes. I presented rather traditional lectures that demonstrated sample searches, and key databases. I would repeat this delivery five times daily in the fall and three times daily in the spring. It was personally exhausting, but even more disconcerting was my growing awareness that the students were not engaged. I did all of the talking while students remained quiet or even fell asleep. No matter what I emphasized in the class, I always ended up repeating the same information to students in follow-up consultation sessions. I became convinced that I needed to present more compelling content in a way that would appear relevant and meaningful.

I remembered a faculty-development session about "just in time" teaching. The idea was for instructors to survey students just before class time to gauge their comprehension of a reading or assignment. The survey allow faculty to plan for classroom activities that are based on the students' immediate and apparent needs. I thought this strategy could set the stage for a conversation about business information instead of a series of product demonstrations.

With the course instructor's support, I introduced myself to students through e-mail a week before my scheduled instruction session, attaching three simple readings on the same topic: market trends in the movie-theater sector. I asked students to read each of the pieces and respond on the course discussion board to the question: "Is a movie theater business a good idea? Why or why not? How do the readings inform your opinion?" The instructor offered the students credit for doing this work.

When I arrived in class, rather than launching into product-demonstration mode, I asked the students by a show of hands who thought a movie theater was a sound business idea and who did not. I then asked why they voted the way they did. Students freely shared their opinions, engaged in a bit of debate——and even the professor chimed in with his own view.

Before I knew it, half the class period was gone. So I transitioned the discussion from opinion sharing into a closer look at the readings and their sources. We talked about reliability and objectivity, bias, and intended audiences. I then asked students to consider what necessary information was still missing to answer the questions. Students correctly called for company and industry information, business-location details, consumer trends, and other competitive-intelligence details.

All of this fed nicely into my wrap-up demonstration of a page on the library website that linked to the most relevant business sources. I assured students that all of the sources would provide access to material similar to the readings we had discussed. Finally, I encouraged students to explore the resources on their own and to consult me if they needed any help.

The class session was positively transformed. Rather than revert-
ing to "sales demo" mode, I actually managed to have a meaningful
conversation with the students. Instead of trying to cram a conversation about business materials into a database demonstration, the
reading assignment front-loaded the examples so that students had
a chance to familiarize themselves with the content beforehand. And
when students come to the library for additional help, I begin the
conversation by referring back to the assigned readings. "Remember
the movie theater report?" I ask. "What we're looking for is a similar
report or trade organization that represents your type of business."
By the time they meet with me for library instruction, students have
at least a foundational idea of the type of material they need, and the
interaction is much more valuable and productive. The method has
proven very engaging, and I have plans to introduce and expand the
tactic in many of my classes.

The Peril of the List

One of the few downsides to the librarian-faculty collaboration is that
the shared enthusiasm can result in a lesson plan that is actually a list of
specific resources. A librarian preparing for a law class, for example, may
have a list like this:

- LexisNexis
- Westlaw
- American Law Reports

Do you really need to teach three similar resources so that students
can be successful with the assignment? Probably not. The pressure of
the one-shot time frame can force teaching librarians to launch right
into technical processes of using resources, while skipping over basic
information literacy concepts necessary to student understanding of
the relevance and usefulness of the resources. Oakleaf, Hoover, et al.
(2012) recommend focusing on the concepts that require explanation (such as the threshold concepts mentioned earlier in this chapter)
and things that "require hands-on practice or discussion and interac-

tion for students to achieve some level of understanding," transferable skills and concepts (7). The underlying concepts are more important than the ins and outs of different databases—save those details for a research guide.

HEY, WHAT HAPPENED TO LEARNING OBJECTIVES?

Though there is a reference to Gilchrist and Zald's method of learning objective design, this chapter does not provide a specific formula for writing learning objectives. Instead, it encourages a way of thinking about your goals for and approach to teaching in a one-shot environment. Learning objectives often address competencies that are expected from an entire course, in which the one-shot is only a part. In fact, most of the course instructors you work with will already have their course learning objectives in place——something you will learn during your instruction interview. There is nothing wrong with writing information literacy learning objectives, per se, but don't get sucked into spending too much time and energy crafting them. The process outlined in this chapter will help you keep your goals reasonable, specific, and student-centered. Keep in mind that in a one-shot session, not all of your goals will be measurable and achievable; information literacy is a complex and messy process, and skills are not always immediately observed——you may not always get to see the "lightbulb" come on, and that's okay!

The extensive taxonomies of educational objectives recommended by Bloom (1956) and Anderson, Krathwhol, and Bloom (2001) are not easily translated to the one-shot environment. However, they do suggest a way of thinking that has been widely adopted in library and training literature by encouraging instructors to think about what you want students to learn and what behaviors will demonstrate their learning. Ask yourself what you want the students to know or be able to do by the end of your session (or more likely, by the end of the course). Your answers to these questions should guide your goals, but don't worry as much about how they are structured. Before you get carried away with a list of goals, remember that this is just one session. You will need to prioritize and focus. For each goal, ask yourself, *So what? Why does this goal matter for this particular class?*

These questions are best posed during your instruction interview with the course instructor (see chapter 2). After you develop your final list of goals for the one-shot session, share them with the instructor. If he or she is expecting miracles, this is a good time to discuss ways to supplement or extend the one-shot (see chapter 7).

Let Go

Ditching the demo is a good place to start, but letting go of tried-and-true practices, even those with little effectiveness, can be a challenge. Letting go can be difficult, but once you try it, you won't want to go back to the old way of doing things. Here are a few other things to consider letting go:

Lose the Script

Though this seems contradictory, you have to plan for serendipity! If you have concocted an exact script of what everyone will do and say, then what room is left for the students' authentic experiences? Make sure you have built in time for students to wrestle with some of the big ideas. Often the procedural details of finding information can be conveyed in other ways such as an online research guide that the students can return to later.

Another problem with a script is the temptation to reuse it for every class. Your goals should be adjusted according to the needs of each individual class. Even if you teach the same section every semester, be sure to revisit and revise; this doesn't mean you have to start from scratch each time, but teaching is a reflective practice—there is always room for improvement. Going without a script does not mean being unprepared; it means being prepared for anything so that you allow space for student involvement. Veldof (2006) suggests you prioritize your "need-to-know" and "nice-to-know" lists (87). Be gentle with yourself if you don't get to it all.

Ignore Bells and Whistles

So you went to a workshop at a conference (or read chapter 4) and found an activity that you can't wait to try? Or perhaps you found a new free technology that seems really nifty. Should you use it? Before you answer that question, go back to your goals. If the new activity or technology will help you efficiently meet those goals, go for it! If it doesn't help you meet your goals, then save it for another time. Student learning should always be the driving force of your plan.

LESSON LEARNED!

Even if an activity or technology will help you meet your goals, consider the cost investment of your time. If you find yourself spending hours designing an interactive game that you will use for five minutes in one class, it may be time to revisit your goals and rethink your plan. Chapter 4 will provide some ideas and guidelines for classroom activities.

Take Off Your Expert Hat

When wearing your expert hat, you are the sage at the front of the room—prepared to tell everyone how to do it the *right* way. Most people are not receptive to being told the right way by someone else. Nor should they be. How many times have you shown students the right way to do research using a specialized database, only to find them on Google during hands-on time? Take off the expert hat and give the students some freedom to take an active role in the class (see chapter 4).

That said, you really are the expert in the room. Unfortunately, in a world where almost everyone has digital access to vast quantities of information, it is easy for people to confuse technological proficiency with information literacy. Chances are the students have little idea what you do. They will value your expertise when they actually experience it, rather than having it imposed on them.

LESSON LEARNED!

Research is an iterative and messy process. As you will see in the next section, students need ample time and support to explore what is out there. Left to their own devices, they are likely to skip the uncomfortable early exploration stages that are necessary to produce a focused, coherent research paper or project. Allow time for the students to muck around a bit using a variety of tools.

Stop Expecting Miracles!

You are planting seeds. Don't expect complete mastery of anything. Students have to put their skills into practice. Make sure the class instructor has realistic expectations too. Be honest with the instructor about the limitations of a one-shot session. The connections you make with the faculty and students are the most fruitful results of a one-shot session—the library session is just the beginning.

Your library colleagues may have unrealistic expectations of your one-shot session too. If you find they are recommending that you "educate" all students about certain services such as interlibrary loan or a food and drink policy, let them know you will be tying all instruction to specific goals for the class and recommend other ways to share services and policies with students.

Timing Really Is Everything
The Right Lesson for the Right Student at the Right Time

Drury's axiom that libraries aspire "to provide the right book for the right reader at the right time" is as true today as it was in 1930. It's an equally reasonable goal to strive to provide the right lesson for the right student at the right time. As mentioned previously, the tricky part is that students are often all over the map in terms of information literacy and knowledge of library resources and services; so how can you design a single lesson that is useful and relevant to all students? Fortunately, the well-researched and widely accepted Information Search Process Model (ISP) identifies six stages that students experience when conducting the information search (Kuhlthau, 2004; Kuhlthau, Heinström, and Todd, 2008). More than two decades of research offers insight into students' thoughts, feelings, and actions at each stage, which gives you the necessary information to identify students' general points of need at the time of the instruction session (see table 3.1).

While the information search process is iterative, successful students generally progress through six stages from the start to finish of a given research assignment: task initiation, topic selection, pre-focus exploration, focus formulation, information collection, and search closure. In order to effectively diagnose the user's information need, Cole, Kennedy, and Carter (1996, 712) further reduce the ISP stages to three: pre-focus stage (Kuhlthau's stages 1, 2, and 3), focus stage (Kuhlthau's stage 4), and post-focus stage (Kuhlthau's stages 5 and 6) (see figure 3.1).

Timing really is everything. There are many aspects of one-shot library instruction that teaching librarians cannot control, so it is only logical to work with something you have some control over—timing. Through the instruction interview (see chapter 2) you can negotiate a date for the library session that makes sense for the assignment and the students' information search process. And designing sessions based on the students' thoughts, feelings, and actions for a targeted phase of the research process will result in instruction that is useful and relevant to the students, which translates into research success. When planning library instruction, careful attention to timing and student needs is critical.

Library instruction for the same assignment should be very different for classes in the early stages of research than those for classes in later stages. For example, explanations, demonstrations, and activities related to creating annotated bibliographies would be welcomed by students in post-focus stages of the research process—who were actually tasked with creating an annotated bibliography at the time the instruction is offered. The same lesson would fall flat for students in pre-focus stages of the research process: simply telling students that the instruction will be useful and relevant in a few weeks or months is not enough to make it feel useful and relevant at the time of instruction.

TABLE 3.1

KUHLTHAU'S MODEL OF THE STAGES OF THE INFORMATION SEARCH PROCESS (KUHLTHAU 2004, 44–50)

Stage 1: Task Initiation

Task	Thoughts	Feelings	Actions	Strategies
To prepare for the decision of selecting a topic	Contemplating assignment Comprehending task Relating prior experience and learning Considering possible topics	Apprehension at work ahead Uncertainty	Talking with others Browsing the library	Brainstorming Discussing Contemplating possible topics Tolerating uncertainty

Stage 2: Topic Selection

Task	Thoughts	Feelings	Actions	Strategies
To decide on topic for research	Weighing topics against criteria of personal interest, project requirements, information available, and time allotted Predicting outcome of possible choices Choosing topic with potential for success	Confusion Sometimes anxiety Brief elation after selection Anticipation of prospective task	Consulting with informal mediators Making preliminary search of library Using reference collection	Discussing possible topics Predicting outcome of choices Using general sources for overview of possible topics

Stage 3: Pre-focus Exploration

Task	Thoughts	Feelings	Actions	Strategies
To investigate information with the intent of finding a focus	Becoming informed about general topic Seeking focus in information on general topic Identifying several possible focuses Inability to express precise information needed	Confusion Doubt . Sometimes threat Uncertainty	Locating relevant information Reading to become informed Taking notes on facts and ideas Making bibliographic citations	Reading to learn about topic Tolerating inconsistency and incompatibility of information encountered Intentionally seeking possible focuses Listing descriptors

Stage 4: Focus Formulation

Task	Thoughts	Feelings	Actions	Strategies
To formulate a focus from the information encountered	Predicting outcome of possible foci Using criteria of personal interest, requirements of assignment, availability of materials, and time allotted Identifying ideas in information from which to formulate focus Sometimes characterized by a sudden moment of insight	Optimism Confidence in ability to complete task	Reading notes for themes	Making a survey of notes Listing possible foci Choosing a particular focus while discarding others, or Combining several themes to form one focus

Stage 5: Information Collection				
Task	**Thoughts**	**Feelings**	**Actions**	**Strategies**
To gather information that defines, extends, and supports the focus	Seeking information to support focus Defining and extending focus through information Gathering pertinent information Organizing information in notes	Realization of extensive work to be done Confidence in ability to complete task Increased interest	Using library to collect pertinent information Requesting specific sources from librarian Taking detailed notes with bibliographic citations	Using descriptors to search out pertinent information Making comprehensive search of various types of materials, i.e., reference, periodicals, nonfiction, and biography Using indexes Requesting assistance of librarian

Stage 6: Search Closure				
Task	**Thoughts**	**Feelings**	**Actions**	**Strategies**
To conclude search for information	Identifying need for any additional information Considering time limit Diminishing relevance Increasing redundancy Exhausting resources	Sense of relief Sometimes satisfaction Sometimes disappointment	Rechecking sources for information initially overlooked Confirming information and bibliographic citations	Returning to library to make summary search Keeping books until completion of writing to recheck information

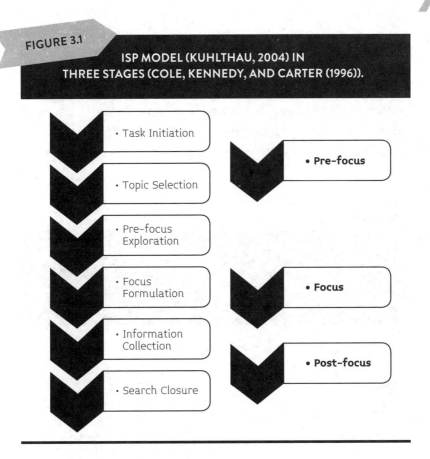

FIGURE 3.1

ISP MODEL (KUHLTHAU, 2004) IN THREE STAGES (COLE, KENNEDY, AND CARTER (1996)).

- Task Initiation
- Topic Selection
- Pre-focus Exploration
- Focus Formulation
- Information Collection
- Search Closure

- **Pre-focus**
- **Focus**
- **Post-focus**

It is noteworthy that one-shot library instruction, especially the database-demonstration approach in the first week of the semester, is often targeted to support post-focus stages, even though most students have not had adequate time and support to process through the pre-focus and focus stages. This timing guarantees a mismatch between what you are teaching, and what they really need, and results in library instruction that is neither relevant nor useful. In fact, there is evidence in the literature that librarian encouragement to form a focus before the student is ready might even be harmful to the student's research process and result in lower-quality research papers (Bodi, 2002; Kennedy, Cole, and Carter, 1999; Nutefall and Ryder, 2010). Students need ample time to explore topics broadly in order to find, focus, and synthesize information.

Time to Teach

For decades, librarians have embraced Kulthau's ISP model as useful for customizing the reference interview. It is an equally powerful tool for customizing the instruction. More specific teaching ideas will be offered in chapter 4, but here are some general suggestions for meeting students at their points of need in the pre-focus, focus, and post-focus stages (see figure 3.2).

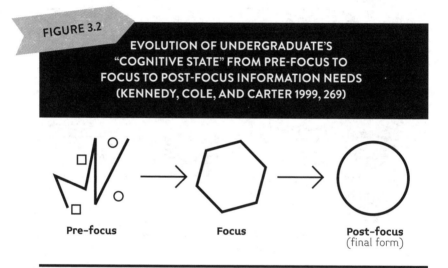

FIGURE 3.2

EVOLUTION OF UNDERGRADUATE'S "COGNITIVE STATE" FROM PRE-FOCUS TO FOCUS TO POST-FOCUS INFORMATION NEEDS (KENNEDY, COLE, AND CARTER 1999, 269)

Pre-focus　　　　**Focus**　　　　**Post-focus**
(final form)

Pre-Focus

At this stage, students are uncertain and apprehensive. With luck they will have already read the assignment, but you should not take anything for granted. It is a wise investment to set aside some time for the students to review the assignment and ask questions of the course instructor.

It is common practice for course instructors to allow students to select their own topics. The well-intentioned idea is that students will choose something that interests them, and thus produce a better paper. This approach often backfires because most students don't have the background knowledge to identify a significant topic. Often their topics are expressed in single word statements, such as "Nursing," or "NASCAR." Bodi (2002, 110) writes:

> It appears that students search in a haphazard, unplanned way, happy to find whatever. In a sense, they are trying to engage in the kind of serendipitous discovery that scholars do, only without having first established the context in which that sort of discovery is likely to happen. In their minds there may be logic to their searching, but the logic is to get a certain quantity of materials because it is shaped by an urgent deadline—hence, the gap between the way librarians teach them to do research and the way they actually do it.

The purpose of library instruction during the pre-focus stage of the research process is to help students establish the context that will lead to focus formulation. Teaching librarians should help students explore broadly and find and use language to talk about potential topics.

LESSON LEARNED!

To facilitate some focus before your class session, ask the class instructor to assign homework before the session to ensure students have done some preliminary topic exploration (see "Vignette: Letting Go of the 'Sales Demo'"). For example, students could be challenged to locate, read, and evaluate in writing one information source. The library session (and the librarian) will be more useful and relevant to students once they have had some struggles with the information search process.

Focus

This stage of the research process is the ideal time to schedule library instruction. Kuhlthau describes it as a "zone of intervention" (Kuhlthau,

1994: 63), because this is a time when students most need a librarian's help. Finding focus is a major stumbling block for most students. Through years of research, Kuhlthau found that half of students failed to find focus (1991, 369) and that without focus, they had difficulty getting through the rest of the assignment (2004, 39).

You cannot artificially force this stage of the research, which is what often happens. If students are still in the pre-focus stage, your instruction should be planned accordingly. If they have had ample time and support to explore, then you can begin to guide them toward focus through surveys of the literature, advanced databases searches, and so on. If at all possible, a workshop model that allows the teaching librarian and course instructor to circulate through the room and work with individual students is best for this stage. The workshop format will enable you to work with the students that need your help the most.

Post-Focus

In this stage, students have reached the stage of their research where the type of traditional library instruction most commonly offered can be relevant and useful. Having arrived at a focus, the student will be receptive to learning about new resources and more advanced search techniques that make searching more precise. They will be ready to earnestly begin to find, evaluate, and use information for their paper or project.

Summary

This chapter deliberately challenges your existing ideas about library instruction. Too often library instruction is teacher-centered, rather than student-centered, with content that is focused on tools and processes rather than basic understandings that are essential for students to grasp in order to be successful with research. Despite the many limitations of one-shot instruction, it can be relevant and useful if taught in a time and manner that meets students at their points of need in the information search process.

CHAPTER 4

"How Do I Get Them to Pay Attention?"
Classroom Strategies for One-Shot Instruction

Fear of public speaking ranks up there with fear of snakes, spiders, and death. Getting up in front of a class of students is nerve-wracking for anyone, but especially for the many introverts who choose librarianship as a profession (Scherdin, 1994). Take a deep breath and relax. You don't have to be the center of attention to be a good teacher. Liberate yourself from the role of presenter and focus instead on being a facilitator of learning. The best teaching is learner-centered and encourages conversation, reflection, and application. It inspires inquiry and discovery while forging a personal and meaningful connection between the learner and the content. Most of all, teaching, when done well, is actually fun. *Here's the catch.* In order to create a learner-centered environment, you have to stop talking, give up some control, and invest time and thought in planning and designing instruction. Armed with good lesson plans, effective teaching strategies, and some practice, you can overcome that pressure to perform and become a better teacher.

This chapter will present tried and true classroom strategies that work well for one-shot instruction. Use a range of activities and approaches to engage students with your learning goals. Though a few of the activities have clever names, they are based on sound pedagogical research. The strategies can be applied to almost any classroom setting and most can also be used as assessment techniques (see chapter 6).

Types of Instruction

Teaching is both an art and a science. There are many different ways to engage students. Some approaches that work well for one-shot instruction are cooperative learning, experiential learning, and direct instruction—or more likely, a combination of all three.

Cooperative Learning

Cooperative learning is teaching that "engages students in collaborative discussions about the content to promote learning" (Stevens 2008, 187). Johnson and Johnson (1999) point out that simply telling a group of students to work together does not qualify as cooperative learning, rather the students should work together toward a common learning goal and have a sense that the success of reaching that goal is dependent on the success of their team members. There are some very sound reasons for cooperative learning or group work. There is safety in numbers for the students, especially when you are presenting them with problems to solve. After all, in a one-shot session, students may be meeting the librarian for the first time, but they may already be used to working with one another. Learning is a social endeavor, so creating a classroom environment allows students to work and learn together. On a practical level, grouping students facilitates the sharing of scarce resources, such as computers.

There are times when the class will already have assigned groups; perhaps they are all preparing for the same debate or presentation. If so, simply ask the students to sit in their pre-assigned groups upon arrival in the classroom. If not, form the groups as the students arrive before class, or mark each seat with a number, colored piece of paper, or brand of candy. The important thing is not to use too many of your precious fifty to seventy-five minutes with logistics. Groups that are assigned on the fly are called "informal cooperative learning groups" and are used to "focus student attention on the material to be learned, set a mood conducive to learning, help organize in advance the material to be covered in a class session, [and] ensure that students cognitively process the material being taught" (Johnson and Johnson 1999, 55). Avoid large groups, which can easily become unwieldy. Beichner (2008) recommends groups of three for effective cooperative learning groups; as one favorite course instructor says, "more than three is a party!"

Active and Experiential Learning

Though the terms *active* and *experiential learning* are often used interchangeably, active learning is an umbrella term that encompasses a variety of student-centered activities while experiential learning incorporates a "practical experience" for the student (Wallace 2009, 99) and includes problem-based and case-based learning. Experiential learning emphasizes true-to-life scenarios and works very well for students in professional programs such as health care, business, and education. Connecting new information to real-world situations can be a very effective way of engaging students—and fortunately for librarians, information literacy is very easy to relate to everyday life. Most of the recommended activities in this chapter will incorporate active or experiential learning.

When first trying active and experiential learning techniques, you may feel uncomfortable. Since you won't be presenting, it may feel like you are not providing enough content. However, if you are observant and responsive you will find ample opportunity to offer students suggestions that are meaningful, relevant, and most importantly, will be gratefully received and remembered.

Direct Instruction

This book challenges you to avoid "covering" the information. The gist is that students don't learn just because you tell them what to do (see chapter 3). However, there are some aspects of traditional direct instruction that are very effective. Hattie (2009) states "too often, what the critics mean by direct instruction is didactic teacher-led talking from the front; this should not be confused with the very successful 'Direct Instruction' method," which is "very successful" (204–05). Instead of just a presentation of information and time for the students to practice, direct instruction requires the instructor to be clear about the goals for the lesson, to "check for understanding" throughout the class session, and to provide "closure"—an opportunity for the class to summarize, review, and ask questions (205–6). The guidelines for direct instruction (clear goals, checks for understanding, and closure) effectively frame any instructional strategy.

Strategies for Student Engagement

Active learning strategies abound. A simple Web search will reveal dozens of websites, many maintained by university- or college-based teaching and learning centers. For the most part college or university faculty developed these strategies when faced with some of the same challenges as teaching librarians trying to engage college students. Fortunately, there are volumes written about instructional strategies. While the strategies presented here are by no means exhaustive, they have been classroom-tested and lend themselves to one-shot instruction.

RESOURCES FOR INSTRUCTIONAL STRATEGIES

Angelo, Thomas A., and K. Patricia Cross. 1993. *Classroom Assessment Techniques: A Handbook for College Teachers*. San Francisco: Jossey-Bass.
Aronson, E., M. Lestik, and S. Plous. *The Jigsaw Classroom: Overview of the Technique*. Retrieved from www.jigsaw.org/overview.htm.
Booth, Char. 2011. *Reflective Teaching, Effective Learning: Instructional Literacy for Library Educators*. Chicago: American Library Association.

Bowman, Sharon L. 2005. *The Ten-Minute Trainer: 150 Ways to Teach It Quick and Make It Stick.* San Francisco: Pfeiffer.

Connor, P. *The Jigsaw Classroom: Building the Big Picture: Master Teacher Initiative Teaching Tips.* Institute for Teaching and Learning at Colorado State University. Retrieved from http://tilt .colostate.edu/tips/tip.cfm?tipid=151.

Cook, D., and R. Sittler. 2008. *Practical Pedagogy for Library Instructors: 17 Innovative Strategies to Improve Student Learning.* Chicago: Association of College and Research Libraries.

Cox, C. N., and E. B. Lindsay. 2008. *Information Literacy Instruction Handbook.* Chicago: Association of College and Research Libraries.

Filene, Peter G. 2005. *The Joy of Teaching: A Practical Guide for New College Instructors.* Chapel Hill: University of North Carolina Press.

McKeachie, W. J. 1990. *Teaching Tips: A Guidebook for the Beginning College Teacher.* Lexington, MA: D.C. Heath.

Morgan, Norah, and Juliana Saxton. 2006. *Asking Better Questions.* 2nd ed. Markham, ON: Pembroke.

Nilson, Linda B. 2010. *Teaching at Its Best: A Research-Based Resource for College Instructors.* 3rd ed. San Francisco: Jossey-Bass.

Tate, M. L. 2004. *"Sit & Get" Won't Grow Dendrites: 20 Professional Learning Strategies That Engage the Adult Brain.* Thousand Oaks, CA: Corwin.

Veldof, Jerilyn R. 2006. *Creating the One-Shot Library Workshop: A Step-by-Step Guide.* Chicago: American Library Association.

Quick and Easy

The following activities don't take a lot of time and are easy to implement anytime throughout the session. They can be used as warm-ups or debriefing (closure), as well as real-time assessment to check in with your students during class.

The One-Minute Paper

A one-minute paper (Angelo and Cross, 1993), also known as the one-minute test or half-sheet response, involves simply asking students to free-write for one minute about a specific topic. Traditionally the technique is used in college classrooms at the end of lectures to provide feedback from the students about the course material. But it is endlessly adaptable, and can be used at any point in a fifty- to 120-minute library instruction session.

For example, in order to activate prior learning and uncover misconceptions about the library, you might prompt students to think about their prior research experiences. Ask students to take out a blank sheet of paper and something to write with. Explain to students that you want them to free-write for one minute. Use a simple question-based prompt, such as: Think back to the last research paper or project you worked on for a class that required you to locate sources of information about your topic. How did it go? What worked? What obstacles did you face? Reassure students that there are no right or wrong answers, and that they will not offend if they share negative experiences.

Allow one to two minutes for students to put their thoughts on paper, and then ask the students to share comments about their experiences. Take time to discuss them with the class. As facilitator, guide the conversation to the types of library resources and services that will help them be successful. Even though the students are initiating the conversation through their one-minute papers, this approach allows you to shape the conversation without dominating it. If you are short on time, you may collect the student responses and sift through them selectively addressing student questions/concerns.

This particular activity is nice to use with incoming freshmen who have little or no experience with a college library. The conversation unfailingly leads to the many differences between a high school library and a college library. It is a way to meet the students where they are and begin your journey together.

Tip: Often, most of the students arrive a few minutes early to class—use this time for the one-minute paper.

Fishbowl

In a fishbowl, a student (or a pair of students) models a certain activity, which can include a discussion or interview. The rest of the class is asked to observe, analyze, and discuss what they have viewed in the fishbowl (Bean 2001, 178). Use this technique carefully in the one-shot setting; students may not enjoy being put on the spot by a relative stranger. One simple version of a fishbowl is to have a small group of students demonstrate a search process in front of the whole class. Ask the class to ask questions and offer constructive suggestions to the search strategy. Give the student presenters uninterrupted time to demonstrate their search, then point out what they did well, and ask the class, "how could this search be improved?" Together with the class, you can make suggestions. In this context, you can slide in your bits of wisdom, but in such a way that honors the students' knowledge and experiences.

Think-Pair-Share

Think-pair-share (Lyman, 1981) is a very simple activity. First, students *think* or free-write independently for two to three minutes about a question or prompt that the librarian has prepared; second, they *pair* with the person sitting next to them to talk about the question or prompt for two to three minutes per person, or five to six minutes per pair; finally students *share* their ideas with the whole class. Think-pair-share is a versatile activity that can be adapted to support students at any stage of the research process and also can be used by the librarian at any time to recapture student attention that has wandered.

Think-pair-share works well as a warm-up activity to encourage students to talk about their topic ideas in the pre-focus stages of the research process. You can prompt students to think-pair-share about possible topics and their significance. Prompts can take the form of a few short questions, with *why* questions being particularly useful to promote critical thinking. For example: What topic or topics interest you? Why are you interested? What do you hope to learn?

While the students are engaged with this activity, walk around the room and observe, making sure to remind students halfway through to give their partner time to talk. Set a timer or an alarm of some sort so you don't have to watch the clock. As students share their topic ideas, record them on the board or poster paper so that you can refer back to the topics and use them for example searches. This approach demonstrates to students that you value them as learners and it invests them in the session. For a twist, during the share part, go around the room round-robin style and have each student introduce their partner's research topic.

Gallery Walk

In a gallery walk, the instructor gives students a prompt (usually a question or set of questions), and asks students to write or draw a response. The participants post their responses on a wall, creating a gallery. Participants walk around to view and comment on or otherwise rate the posters, using sticky notes or stickers. Gallery walks are particularly helpful in assessing your participants' needs at the beginning of a session or debriefing at the end of the session—it's a useful way to gather information quickly (Bowman, 2005). Gallery walks also provide the opportunity for peer review, whole class engagement, and getting the students up and moving around. You may have participated in a gallery walk yourself; the technique is very popular with trainers and facilitators.

For example, Bowman suggests using gallery walks at the beginning of class to invite students to help set the agenda for the day's session. Ask students to anonymously post something they want to learn about to the classroom wall. You should give examples, such as Web evaluation, finding scholarly articles, or narrowing down a topic. Give each student three star stickers and ask them to use the stickers to vote for what they want or need to learn that day. This activity can help students define their own information needs.

Gallery walks could just as easily be used at the end of a class session to provide closure for the day's activities (Bowman 2005). For example, individually or in teams, have students post a reflection about something new they learned in class. Just as above, conclude the activity with a walk for students to view each other's reflections and vote by sticker on those they agree with most. If there is time, have a group discussion about what the students discovered during their walk.

Concept Maps and Graphic Organizers

Graphic organizers and concept maps help students visualize relationships between concepts. In information literacy, concept maps are often used for topic brainstorming or thinking about the structure of information. Radcliff et al. (2007) recommend concept maps for thinking about "research strategy, [the] publication cycle, types of information resources for specific disciplines, and evaluation of information resources for authority" (107). For example, you could ask students to create a flow chart to illustrate how they would go about evaluating a source. This activity allows students to think outside the checklist.

To save time in your one-shot session, instead of having students start their concept map from scratch, you can provide some of the structure and ask them to fill in the blanks. A popular example of this is a KWL (know/ want to know/learned; see figure 4.1). A KWL helps you structure a workshop when the students are still in their pre-focus stages (see chapter 3). This also serves as a "snapshot" assessment tool for the librarian and the classroom instructor to be able to see at a glance where a student is with his or her topic, and pinpoint those who need more assistance.

Here's how the KWL works:

- At the start of a research workshop class, ask students to use a KWL graphic organizer to write down what they know in the appropriate space or column of the KWL.
- Next, ask them to write about what they want to know in the appropriate space or column of the KWL.
- Allow students time to search for needed information, using a research guide or other resources gathered together. Ask them to make notes about what they learned in the appropriate space or column of the KWL.
- As they work, walk around the room, answer questions, and look at the KWLs. If it appears a student is struggling, use the KWL to find out more about the student's approach and identify ways to help him or her.

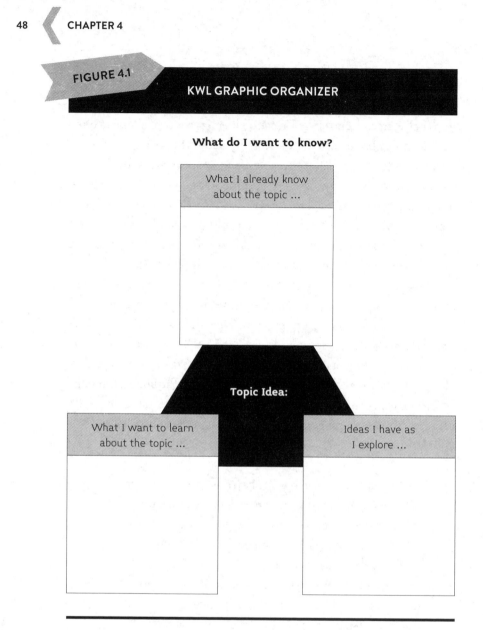

FIGURE 4.1

KWL GRAPHIC ORGANIZER

What do I want to know?

What I already know about the topic ...

Topic Idea:

What I want to learn about the topic ...

Ideas I have as I explore ...

More Complex Activities

The following activities will work in a one-shot session, but will take most or all of the class session and require more preparation ahead of time. Each activity engages students in cooperative and experiential learning.

The Jigsaw

The jigsaw can seem complicated at first, but it is one of the most effective ways to structure cooperative, engaged learning even with larger classes. The activity was originally designed as a cooperative learning strategy to promote intergroup relations in the classroom during the desegregation era (Aronson, 1978). Today it is widely used for active learning. It's a great tool to get students to learn and share information about library resources and services. Like a jigsaw puzzle, each student's part is important to final understanding of the complete material.

As with all of these activities, the jigsaw can be adapted to fit a variety of teaching and learning needs at various stages of the research process. During the early stages, it is useful as a tool for students to orient themselves to library services and resources. For example, if students are ready to collect information in earnest, a jigsaw might be used to familiarize them with information in an online research guide. Put the students in expert groups and have each expert group learn about one section of the research guide. Midway through the session, have students reconfigure into sharing groups, made up of at least one expert on each section of the research guide. The experts then teach each other about the sections of the research guide, assembling the information as one would a jigsaw puzzle. A main goal for this example is to point students to the existence and purpose of the information in the research guide without a "point and click" demonstration. Each student will get to explore and experience a particular aspect of the research guide and share it with others. As they share, their peers can think about the different resources and types of information available and which ones might work for them. By teaching the topic, the students take ownership of the material.

If you have a small class or are a little nervous about the logistics of the jigsaw, you can do a half jigsaw (Reeves, McMillan, and Gibson, 2008) and have expert teams present to the whole class from the teacher station. Half jigsaws save a little time and give you a chance to chime in with your own advice.

Tip: Make sure your instructions for the jigsaw are clear. You may want to provide specific questions or tasks to give the experts something concrete to share or explain.

LESSON LEARNED!

Because jigsaws involve two different groups, they can be confusing to implement. This is especially true when you never know how many students are actually going to show up. Using colored paper to assign jigsaw topics really helps. Before the class, print out or copy a list of the topics on each of the different colored papers and cut them in strips so that each member of your sharing groups will have the same color strip of paper, but each with a different topic. Form your expert groups by calling out the name of the topic, and your sharing groups by calling out the color. Figure 4.2 illustrates sixteen participants in their expert groups and figure 4.3 shows the same participants in their sharing groups. During the jigsaw activity you should drop in on the groups, perhaps just to listen or to offer clarification and answer questions. Conclude the activity with whole class discussion.

FIGURE 4.2

EXPERT GROUPS

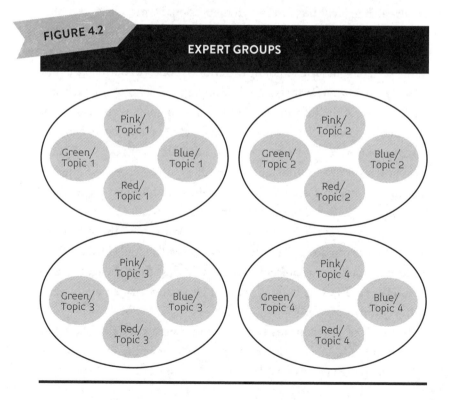

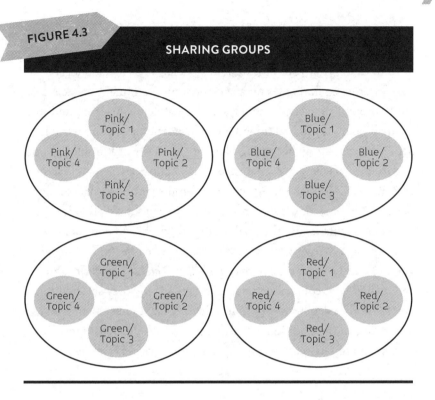

FIGURE 4.3

SHARING GROUPS

Case Studies

Case studies are narratives of real-life scenarios, but more importantly they provide a problem that students need to solve. Nilson (2010) advises that in addition to providing real-life examples, cases should provide "opportunities for synthesis"—students should be able to apply what they are learning to solve the case (183). In a one-shot session, in order to avoid the lecture/demo and allow students time to work on a case study, you may want to provide additional information, such as a research guide, that students can consult as they work on the case. Cases, according to Nilson, also involve "uncertainty" and "risk" (i.e., they should allow for "multiple solutions and valid debate," and the students should understand why solving the case is important) (2010, 183). In an information literacy setting, there are often multiple solutions and approaches to the same end; case studies should emphasize the process for solving the problem. If you use a case study, be explicit about its relevance both to real life and to the research the students have to do for the class.

For example, if you want students in a law class to use a legal database in order to find cases on a specific topic, you might create a case study prompt or scenario about a college athlete who is injured in a football game. Try to find something in recent news for your example to avoid the case study becoming like the generic "word problems" you had to solve in elementary math class (e.g., Train A is leaving the station at 2:30 . . .). Though uncertainty is an important element, you don't have a lot of time for the students to work, so you should provide details to help students focus. The final prompt might be: *You are an attorney representing a college, where an athlete is injured on the field at a football game. Locate two legal cases that would help you advise your client.* Later in the session, you could ask students to defend why they selected those cases—and explain how they found them. Case studies can be a logical alternative to the traditional research project, so the course instructor may be interested in turning this activity into a class assignment.

Role Play

Role play and case studies often overlap. For instance, in the example above, students are playing the role of an attorney. Role playing usually involves more outward acting; it encourages improvisation and creativity and "allows students to experience issues both affectively and cognitively" (Collins and O'Brien 2003, 308). There are a lot of possibilities for role play, but for your one-shot session, you will want to keep it simple. For example, you might assign each person in a small group a specific role—one could drive the shared computer, one could navigate the research process, and a third could record the findings. (See chapter 5 for some interesting options for role play in a learning management system.) The vignette in this chapter involves simple role play. A more elaborate example could be asking a group of journalism students to play fact-checkers for a magazine by using quality sources to confirm certain factual statements in an article (lengthy, fact-filled articles from publications like *The Atlantic* or *New Scientist* work the best); if time allows, students can take turns as copy editor pointing out factual errors to their "reporters" and guiding them to the best sources. This type of role play empowers students to be critical of information sources, and is another example of an activity that could become a class assignment. Another popular, and more physical, role play is to have students act out the parts of a citation (author, title, etc.) and organize themselves in proper order according to their style guide. After the role play, the librarian can discuss the parts of the citation and talk more in depth about different types of information.

Like case studies, role plays allow for some flexibility in the student's response and provide a "what if" scenario for the student to really think through possible solutions (Bean 2001, 156). Students may be shy about performing in front of you, their instructor, and their peers; be sure to talk to the instructor about the class culture before designing a role play activity. Some students will be suited to more sedentary role plays such as the fact-checker example; other classes will be up for more improvisation and action. For the one-shot session, role play often works best in pairs or small groups. A couple of brave students may be willing to model their role play for the whole group (see "Fishbowl" earlier in this chapter).

Games

Games can engage students and inspire motivation, but sometimes, in an effort to make the session fun, it can be easy to lose sight of the actual goals for the class. Millis and Cotell advise that "any game activity must be preceded by clear explanations, including a careful rationale linked to course goals" (1998, 150). It's nice if your students look back on your session as fun, but more importantly, they should look back on your class as helpful, relevant, and enlightening.

Games often encourage a problem-based approach or involve a simulation such as role playing. You can easily turn an activity into a game by asking students to compete against each other or by giving prizes at the end. For any game, keep the competitive aspect low-risk; if students "lose" the game, they are only missing out on a sticker or piece of candy. Simulations and more elaborate games are popular in the library literature, but should only be used when they are the best way to accomplish some of your goals. Bingo and Jeopardy are popular games because they provide a template for connecting your learning goals to a game that most students have played or watched before; they can be a fun way to introduce or review basic facts and concepts before moving on to more complex ideas. Since you are preparing for a one-shot session, be sure to weigh your time investment with the possible reward. If you are hankering to try an online game, there are some pre-designed information literacy games online that could be used in class (ACRL's Primo database indexes some good ones). Or you could assign a game as "homework" before class to introduce some basic concepts or skills; playing a game before class might be more appealing to students than watching a tutorial.

A Word about Scavenger Hunts

Every librarian has a horror story about scavenger hunts. Though always well intentioned (and often initiated by the class instructor), these activities usually require dogged determination rather than information literacy skills. If you want to get to students to get to know the library, create authentic experiences (e.g., have them look up a book on *their* topic and go get it) instead of asking them to chase down an esoteric encyclopedia entry. Pass this tip along to course instructors.

Structured Workshop

If the students are in the throes of their research, the best activity can be working on their own project. It's a good idea to provide some structure—specific instructions and expectations. For example, by the end of class, students should have basic background information about their topic, or locate an advocacy or professional organization related to the topic, or locate news articles related to their topic. Instead of giving the students a handout with a list of suggested resources, encourage the students to record their process throughout the workshop, writing down the resources, search terms, and so on that worked best for their individual topics. The possibilities are boundless, but you should examine their assignment carefully so that you structure the workshop in such a way that it will be meaningful and relevant.

For example, you could ask the students individually or in groups to locate one resource on the Web about their topic. Then, you could do the same thing for a reference source and a scholarly article. Allow the students some freedom to choose databases, search engines, and other resources to use—you will learn a lot by observing their different approaches. Walk around the room while they are searching and make sure they are finding relevant information, and provide guidance when necessary. Wrap up the workshop with a discussion about the features of each type of source and how each could be used in academic research. As a class group, make a list of strategies and tools for finding more relevant resources. This list can be posted to a research guide after class so students can refer back to it. As with other problem-based activities, keep the introduction brief and leave plenty of room at the end of class for debriefing and questions.

At first this loose approach can be uncomfortable, because you may feel pressured to exert more control over the content of the session and discussion. For example, you might want to impress upon students that some types of sources are better than other types of sources, but resist that temptation. Provide advice and guidance when it is needed, but allow students to critically reflect on their own authentic experiences. And just as with any of these activities, you can effectively steer from the sidelines without dominating.

COMMON MISHAPS AND WHAT TO DO ABOUT THEM

The Surfer

Sometimes, no matter how exciting and dynamic your class sessions are, there will still be a student or two who doesn't want to engage. It can often be very tempting for the student to check e-mail, work on another assignment, text a friend, take a nap, and so on. The next time you are in a meeting or workshop with your colleagues, take a look around—librarians do it too! Here are some ways to deal with (or prevent) the surfer.

Ask the class instructor to introduce you and emphasize the importance of the library session. This should be part of the planning process with the instructor.

At the beginning of class, ask them to turn off phones, Facebook, and other possible distractions. Keep the computers off (or frozen if you have classroom control software) until you need them.

For collaborative activities, assign each person a "role" with some sort of responsibility.

Incorporate an activity that does not require use of a computer (gallery walk, think-pair-share, role play, etc.).

If students aren't paying attention while you are speaking, scan the room. If it is just one student surfing/texting, continue speaking while you go and stand by that student for a few seconds. You can be subtle about this. There's no need to shame the student—your close presence should do the trick. If several students aren't paying attention, it's time to stop talking and move on to something else.

Let it go. If a student is still not paying attention, don't worry about it. Students have to take ownership for their educational experience. If a student is truly being disruptive, ask the course instructor to intervene.

The Repeat Customer

You have made efforts to strategically place and scaffold library instruction throughout the curriculum, yet every semester you will have a student or two who has been in every one of your workshops. The key in this situation is to identify them as soon as possible. Ideally, you can do this in advance by asking the instructor to poll the class. More realistically, you can poll the class as they are arriving. Sometimes you will recognize the student (or you will hear *oh, not this again!*) Once you have identified the repeat customers, welcome them back and let them know you will be doing something that will add on to what they've learned before. Then give them some extra responsibility as "co-teachers"——if you have a demo planned, ask them to "drive," or ask them to be your timekeepers, pass out handouts, or assist other students. When you form groups, assign the repeat customers to groups of newcomers.

You Run Out of Time
This will happen a lot. The sooner you accept that the session will not go perfectly according to plan, the more you will enjoy teaching. There are a few things that will help you with pacing.

Post an agenda: this suggestion is common in the training literature because a posted agenda clearly communicates your plan with the participants, who can help you stay on task.

Use a timekeeper: you can assign this role to a person (see "The Repeat Customer" above) or you can use a timer (buy a cheap egg timer, or use a timer on a computer, cell phone, or watch).

Plan for chaos: build plenty of "wiggle room" into your session and always leave room at the end for debriefing and review, even if you have to skip part of an activity.

It's a good idea to remind students at the end of class that you are available for additional one-on-one or group research appointments.

Ok, You Can Talk . . . a Little!

Throughout this book, we have encouraged you to ditch the demo, and to stop talking. This is to prevent the following outcomes:

- The session would have gone exactly the same way if students were not in the room.
- A specific vendor would hire you to do the exact same presentation to potential customers.

- You get tired of hearing your own voice.
- Students think of your class as a "good time to catch up on (Facebook, homework, nap time, etc.)."

But, of course, you will need to talk a little. Even if you spend most of your time facilitating activities, you will still need to give instructions and examples, provide opportunities for reflection, and offer students some closure. Naturally, this will involve some speaking, and probably some demonstration. Veldof suggests peppering short three- to seven-minute "lecturettes" throughout the session (2006, 101); this is a good approach to direct instruction rather than long introductory lectures. When you do speak, continue the theme of connecting the information to students' experiences. With this in mind, it may be best to do most of your talking and showing toward the end of class, after the students have had time to explore the information; it will be easier to facilitate discussion among the students and you will be able to include concrete tips and tricks because the students will already have some experience with the skill, resource, or concept.

When you do speak, avoid jargon (or at least clearly define it) and keep your explanations brief. Ken Bain's (2004) interviews with the "best college teachers" suggest that "the most successful communicators treated anything they said . . . as a conversation rather than a performance" (118). Bain also found that tone was an important component: "the best professors tended to use warm language, to be explicit, to be complete, and to tell the story and make the explanation.... They would bring their listeners inside the material" (122–23). In other words, rattling off instructions to "click here" and "go there" is not very helpful, especially since with the rapid pace of change, those instructions will probably be different by next week. Instead, any speaking that you do should help students understand *why* they should "click" around a particular resource or use a certain skill; this will help you address some of the threshold concepts described in chapter 3.

The storytelling approach appeals to a lot of librarians, because using stories, analogies, and humor to explain concepts is a good way to connect the information to students' existing experiences. Keep analogies simple, for instance comparing a call number to a street address. Avoid elaborate analogies, which can be even more difficult to absorb than the concept itself. Also be aware of your audience—many, for example, may never have used a telephone book, so that may no longer be a good analogy for subject headings. Try to tell stories that are understandable to the general population, rather than a specific gender, age group, or discipline.

LESSON LEARNED!

Don't try to connect to things with which you have no experience. For example, when using a reference to popular music, make sure the reference *naturally flows into the classes' subject matter.* And only use the reference if you actually listen to this music yourself. Otherwise, you will feel like a phony, and the students will be able to tell. Think back to your favorite teachers in school; they probably had their own unique style and way of expressing themselves, and didn't try to mimic or pander to their students.

Classroom Discussion

Asking open-ended questions at the very beginning of the class can result in a chorus of crickets or perhaps a couple answers from the same person—or worse, the librarian will end up answering his or her own questions to fill the silence! Morgan and Saxton (2006) advise instructors not to ask questions if the "students have insufficient knowledge and experience from which to draw an answer" (90). They also advise instructors to give students time to think about the question. In a one-shot environment, it is often more effective if the students discuss with one another, instead of the whole group, at least in the beginning. If you want the students to think about a question or issue at the beginning, activities such as the one-minute paper or think-pair-share will allow time for each individual to think about and answer that question. Then you can open the sharing time to the whole class.

Quality discussion depends on a quality prompt. Prompts should ask students to talk about something they already know. They should challenge students to think critically: instead of asking a question like, "What is Wikipedia?" ask questions like "What does Wikipedia do well?" or "Why don't some of your instructors want you to use Wikipedia?" Morgan and Saxton also warn against asking "leading questions" (2006, 97). An example of a leading question is, "Why is Wikipedia an unreliable source?"

VIGNETTE: TEACH THEM TO THINK FIRST
—*Krista Schmidt, Research and Instruction Librarian, Liaison to Math, Science, and Engineering, Western Carolina University*

Over the years, I've noticed the tendency of students to think very narrowly about their topics and plunge into the literature without engaging in much strategic thinking. I decided to help them break out of that rut by creating a student-to-student interview. I paired students and had them interview each other about their topics based on a set of questions I wrote. There were several reasons I had them interview one another: first, I wanted to allow the interviewee to free-form think without having to worry about remembering what he or she actually said; and second, I didn't want the interviewee to focus on getting the phrasing, wording, or sentence structure to look nice. I also hoped that the interviewer would ask the interviewee to expound or clarify their thoughts. Though this approach was somewhat successful, I was still dissatisfied with the depth of their inquiry. One day when I was helping a student who had missed the information literacy session, I encouraged him to think beyond the formal one-sentence proposal students seem inclined to recite when asked about their research. I hit the jackpot when I asked him to "explain it to me like I am your mom." This tactic worked by helping the student identify larger, simpler concepts that could be used together with their more esoteric terms.

I thought that the explain-it-to-your-mom technique had real potential so I incorporated it into the interview questions for an undergraduate chemistry class. These chemistry students were asked to design their own lab procedure based on an instructor-created problem. Because the problem was succinctly defined already, the students tended to think narrowly about their topic. But finding relevant information can be problematic when the student hasn't taken time to think through what he or she is looking for. I wanted the interview to be used as a thinking assist. Two particular questions that I had the students use for the interview seemed to work well at getting students to think:

How would you explain these concepts in other ways? For example, if you had to explain what your experiment is about to your mom or dad, what would you say? How would you describe it to them?

What don't you know at this point (besides exactly how you are going to perform this experiment)? What's unclear?

This strategy prompted students to think and write down what they knew, what they didn't, and what they might do next. The initial searches they did were more targeted than those I had encountered in previous sessions working with classes on the same assignment.

I plan to continue using the interview as a focus tool for students, especially in my advanced classes, though I'm concerned that the students didn't seem to be naturals at interviewing each other. Many of the students continue to take what they are told at face value without questioning it or seeking clarification. The provoking, questioning, and challenging that leads to more strategic thinking was still not what I hoped. In the future I plan to try modeling the interview process for them before the activity to encourage them to question and respond more deeply.

Getting Them to Ask You Questions

In a one-shot session, it can be a challenge to get the students to ask you questions. Again, you will probably have more luck when the students are working on an activity. If you are milling about the room, observing and coaching, the students can ask you questions if they run into problems. Morgan and Saxton (2006) recommend that the instructor quietly observe the students while they are working instead of interrupting the students while they are in the midst of problem-solving. Try to wait for the student to ask you for help, and if you see several students grappling with the same problems, you can address the questions with the entire class during your review.

Sometimes it becomes clear that more follow-up is needed. Perhaps the students need more guided practice, or they've come up with questions you can't answer right away. If a few individuals need more help, you may want to get their e-mail addresses or schedule some one-on-one appointments. You can also encourage them to visit the reference desk for assistance as well. Some librarians feel that if the students come to the reference desk after a library instruction session, it means the session was ineffective. Quite the contrary; it means they know when to ask an expert for help and they know how and where to go for assistance. If it seems the students need a follow-up class session, discuss this need with the instructor; this may be an inroad to a more embedded model.

Summary

You don't have to be a dynamic presenter to engage students in an interesting and informative one-shot. There are many different methods to create an active and cooperative learning environment ranging from quick and easy exercises to more elaborate activities. It's okay for you to talk and demonstrate, but be sure the students have a chance to speak up and ask questions. Modify and adapt the strategies and suggestions to your own situation and learning goals. Don't be frustrated if your class does not go perfectly according to plan; even the best, most seasoned teachers experience mishaps and embrace them as a learning opportunity.

"But My Classroom Is (Online, in an Auditorium, in a Classroom with No Computers)"

We all have our dream classroom settings, but sometimes life has other plans. Teaching librarians provide one-shot sessions to all kinds of classes, at all levels and all subjects—and in a variety of settings. Situations often arise that force you out of your comfort zone. In the face of unusual challenges, you might be tempted to fall back on the "demo" model. Don't. You can still conduct learner-centered instruction in less-than-perfect settings. If you communicate clearly with the course instructor and have a good plan based on what you want the students to learn, you can use similar practical pedagogy as you would use for any of your other classes—you just have to adapt your approach (and your attitude). This chapter will give you some tips for planning and teaching classes in three different situations: online, in an auditorium, and in a classroom with no computers. Many of the suggestions in this chapter are detailed in chapter 4.

CHAPTER 5

But My Classroom Is Online

Much of the library literature discusses asynchronous strategies such as following online discussions, answering relevant research questions, and posting supplemental materials such as online modules, video tutorials, and research guides. These asynchronous methods can be used as approaches to supplementing one-shot instructions (see chapter 7), but the true parallel to the one-shot session in an online environment takes place synchronously.

The instructional strategies you choose to use online will depend on the tools provided by the learning management system (LMS), or lack thereof, as well as which tools the course instructor and students are accustomed to working with. The 2010 Campus Computing Project (2010) reports that the majority of all colleges or universities have an LMS, with most using either Blackboard or Moodle. Your institution may also provide web conferencing capability, which may or may not be built into the LMS. Web conferencing is also easily accessible through free or inexpensive online tools.

SYNCHRONOUS LEARNING VS. ASYNCHRONOUS LEARNING

Synchronous learning: A learning process in which instructor and students interact simultaneously via an online program. It takes place in a virtual classroom through video conferencing or Web-based real-time broadcasting.

Asynchronous learning: The education of students at different times and locations, often called "anytime, anyplace learning." Asynchronous learning involves the ability to maintain communication without having to meet at the same place at the same time through a common conference space (e.g., bulletin board, e-mail, chat room) available where everyone can post a message, read a message, or respond to a message all within the same shared space. A learning process in which interactions between instructors and students occur with a time delay so students can self-pace their own learning process (Collins and O'Brien, 2003).

Planning and Preparing Your Session
Collaborate

As always, collaboration with course instructors is critical to your success. When teaching online, there's a chance that the instructor will not be in the same room (or even the same state) as you are. Here are some questions to add to your instruction interview with the course instructor:

- What online course tools do you use to teach?
- What is the class culture—how do the students communicate with you and each other?
- Have the students ever used [insert your ideal communication venue, such as Web conferencing here]?
- Do the students work in groups?
- What log-ins or permissions will I need? How far in advance will I get access to the LMS?
- May I post some tutorials/modules/information in advance of the session, and will you require your students to look at the information before class?
- Would you be willing to ask the students to do some homework before our session?

Remember that just as in your face-to-face classes, the course instructor should be required to be an active participant in the session.

Try to get a sense of what tools the course instructor uses with the class on a regular basis. You need to plan for how much direction the students will need to engage in your session and try to minimize any potential technological disruption that might be caused by student inexperience.

Train

Technical difficulties are an oft-cited hurdle for synchronous online instruction; if possible, take advantage of the venues that the students and instructors already know and use. Get any training you might need well in advance. *Tip*: Even if you are already savvy with the software, go to the training sessions your institution provides—it's a chance to demonstrate to the course instructors once again that you are an equal partner in educational success and you are willing and able to be a part of an online class. Plus, you will often be able to make positive and helpful contributions to the session from your perspective as a librarian.

Get Your Gear Together

Plan for the types of equipment you will need for the session (headphones, microphone, Web camera, etc.). Also, think through the resources that you want to make available, including your contact information. If you are going to embed a tutorial or a video, make sure everything works well in advance.

Practice!

Establish a comfort level with the technology so you can focus on teaching and learning. Many LMS administrators can set you up in a test environment, or you can use conferencing software to conduct a run-through. It's better to discover in advance that, for example, your computer's built-in microphone can create strange audio feedback that will disrupt the session. Ask your colleagues to pretend they are your students (if possible, send someone to a place without high-speed Internet); their feedback will help you work out some of the kinks.

Assign Prep Work

Before your synchronous session, Ko and Rossen (2010) recommend posting information including an agenda and any assignments that will help the students prepare. You or the course instructor should post clear instructions to the course shell that students check regularly. Assigning prep work also gives the students a connection to you before the synchronous session. You could ask the students to view a video clip, go through a tutorial or module (try Primo or Merlot for existing tutorials), read an article, take a survey, or do an activity before the synchronous session. This helps you identify where the students are and it helps them be ready to engage in the session.

Plan for Chaos

Problems with technology might (and probably will) happen. You will need a back-up plan for small glitches in the technology—for instance, can you use text chat if the audio doesn't work? But if half the class can't effectively participate, just reschedule.

Teach, Don't Train

Creating a dynamic and interactive classroom in an online environment can be challenging. Resist the urge to fall back on lecture and demo or "vendor webinar" methods. You can use effective, engaging teaching strategies in the online environment. You will find that some things might be easier with an LMS (addressing the students by name, polling for feedback, getting more individuals to participate in discussion), but you will have to adjust other approaches—and your thinking.

Invite Student Participation

Most learning management systems allow for group work. This is one thing you will want to organize in advance with the instructor. You will want to try using methods that the students already know or are easy to learn. Here are a few easy features for collaboration:

- Chat—Most online courses have some sort of chat, collaboration, or Web conferencing feature, either built in or added to the learning management system. Students can ask questions throughout the class or can chat with one another. They can post their questions without disrupting the flow of the session. They can ask questions of each other and clarify things for each other. Chat is a synchronous activity that can generate discussion/questions at the same time because people don't have to wait for a break in the conversation to contribute. Chat is great for think-pair-share activities and for checking in with your students when they are working independently.

- Discussion boards—Discussion boards are an excellent vehicle for cooperative learning groups. In Blackboard, students can self-enroll in groups by research area or groups can be randomly assigned. Groups can also be set up manually. Check with the instructor to see if he or she already uses groups; existing groups will have an established rapport and you won't waste any time with the setup.

- Journals and blogs—Most learning management systems have journal or blog features. Journals and blogs can be set up to be viewable by the whole class or private to a group or just the student and instructors. They provide a good venue for free-writing activities such as the one-minute paper (chapter 4).

- Wikis—Use a page that all students can contribute to as a group activity. Ask students to post recommended resources and search strategies with an explanation of why they made a particular recommendation. If your

LMS doesn't have a wiki feature, find a free option. If your institution has LibGuides, you can incorporate some of the "user input" features such as link suggestion and comments into your research guide.

LESSON LEARNED!

If you have a whole class contribute to a wiki, set up a template to provide some structure. For example, how many types (not formats) of information can you find about your career?

Newspaper article
Trade magazine article
Encyclopedia entry
Government document
Professional organization

Then the student, team, or group can find example sources and hyperlink, add annotations, and so on.

Engage

Many of the student engagement strategies discussed in chapter 4 are effective and employable in the online environment. Here are some to try:

- The one-minute paper: Students can post their papers to a discussion board, a journal or blog (see above), or send them to you privately (via the LMS or e-mail). Angelo and Cross's *Classroom Assessment Techniques* (see chapter 6) such as the one-sentence summary and muddiest point are other options.

- Structured workshop: As in the face-to-face sessions, if students are in the focus or post-focus stages of research, a workshop that allows them to spend time on their individual research is often a good bet. The trick in the online environment is to find ways of checking in with the students. The chat or whiteboard features can help you field questions as they come up (see the *Tip* below). Give the students something concrete they have to report toward the end of the session.
- Case studies (see chapter 4): Post the case study and instructions before your one-shot meeting so students can start thinking about it ahead of time.
- Games: Keep games simple; a Web conferencing or chat feature may make a quiz-type game a bit easier. For example, you could provide slides with questions and students can "ring" in with their answer via a chat feature. Just as with any one-shot, consider your time investment; don't spend hours designing a game that will be played once for five minutes.
- Fishbowl: This activity asks the students to model certain skills while their classmates watch. With many LMSs and Web conferencing software, students can share their screens with the entire class. If your technology is advanced enough to do this, Finkelstein (2006) recommends a "solo fishbowl" (107). In this activity, "learners are given a portion of a shared workspace or whiteboard where they work independently to respond to a problem or complete a task while in the virtual presence of a small group of peers" (107).
- Role play: For a twist on role play, and a way to give a special assignment to a "repeat customer" (see chapter 4), you can assign a special role to one of your students. Finkelstein (2006) recommends various "sidekick roles" that are fun for the participant and help you with classroom management (87):

○ The "voice of the web" (87): If you are employing live chat, whiteboard, or discussions you may want to assign this role, whose responsibility is to keep an eye on communication throughout the class and make sure everyone gets to participate and everyone stays on task. Share this task with a colleague or the course instructor. If it is your first online class, bring in someone who is very familiar with the technology you are using.

○ "Designated skeptic" (87): It can often be hard to gauge what students are really thinking about the presentation, especially if, as Finkelstein points out, you can't hear the sighs or see eyes rolling. The designated skeptic has the role of being the voice of dissent: "the skeptic is urged to use available tools to voice disagreement, confusion, or questions" (87). The assigned skeptic could communicate via a chat feature that is open to the entire class or communicate directly with the librarian via a one-on-one chat, e-mail, or even telephone.

○ "Studio audience" (88): Finkelstein suggests having a group of people who are physically present with you while you are teaching your online class. This group "provides [the] instant nonverbal, visual, and auditory feedback" that you may not get from your online participants. If you are teaching a hybrid class, you have a ready-made studio audience, or you can bring in some coworkers who are curious about online teaching.

Tip: Use quiet time and debriefing time. Most of these activities will have some downtime while students are working on their own or discussing with one another. The silence on your end will feel strange at first, but you can check in with students throughout the session and debrief with the whole class at the end. Use a chat function or whiteboard for students to ask questions as they are working or use polling software to check for understanding. The students can use screen-sharing capabilities to demonstrate what they have learned to the whole class or students could also contribute to a wiki, blog, or shared online research guide, which the whole group could discuss during the debriefing. Finkelstein's sidekick roles listed above, such as the "studio audience" and the "voice of the web," are clever ways of dealing with the silence and keeping you on task.

VIGNETTE: TAKING IT ONLINE IN REAL TIME
—Bianca Rivera, Valencia College

I began offering real-time online library instruction two years ago. I was frustrated with not being able to teach distance students the same way I teach on-campus students. I wasn't satisfied with asynchronous, static tutorials and wanted to duplicate the live, face-to-face library instruction experience for online students.

I reached out to our campus IT to see what help they could offer me and learned about the availability of new online conferencing software. I found the software intuitive to use and quickly learned how to offer my own virtual library instruction sessions. I recorded these sessions so students that did not attend could still benefit from the presentation.

Utilizing the software, students could watch me demonstrate how to use electronic resources and ask questions at their point of need. They were also able to demonstrate their skills for their classmates as the software allowed for screen, keyboard, and mouse sharing. To my surprise, students did not hesitate to share their screens, ask questions when they are confused, and participate when I facilitated group discussion. Some students have even used their webcams during the sessions!

The results have been encouraging. In the two years since I have started this project, eight faculty members have regularly incorporated virtual library instruction into their courses. Unfortunately, as these are asynchronous online classes, attendance cannot be made mandatory and so has varied from a low of one to a high of twenty-nine students per session. I have hypothesized potential reasons for this, such as faculty not posting the session details early enough; students' personal schedules not being able to accommodate the sessions; and of course, the all too common lack of student interest. In response to low turnout during the day sessions, I have now moved the sessions to the evenings, starting at 6 or 7 pm. Also, I have found that many students opt to watch the recordings rather than attending live.

One challenge is that not all instructors attend the virtual sessions. Although the library requires course instructors to attend all face-to-face library instruction sessions, I think some instructors believe that because this is a virtual presentation they do not have to attend class with their students. However, I find greater student participation and engagement when the professor is also in attendance. Students seem very relieved that the professor is there to answer questions. As I fine-tune the online sessions in the future, this will certainly be an issue I address.

But My Class Is in an Auditorium

If you are teaching a one-shot in an auditorium, it probably means that the class is too big to meet anywhere else. The theater-like setting can induce the pressure to perform, but resist! You can adapt your active and collaborative teaching strategies to this setting too. In fact, cooperative and active learning techniques are often recommended strategies for large classes. Below are some general recommendations for an auditorium-based class.

Recruit Help

You can handle a huge class if you need to, but if you prefer to mill about the classroom and work closely with the students, ask for help. Also, with a huge class, taking on a more elaborate activity, such as a jigsaw, can make you feel like a circus ringmaster. Find a colleague (a fellow teaching librarian, a stellar student worker, the library director) to help coordinate groups and check in with the students. If you have a "repeat customer" as described in chapter 4, give that student a role as a helper. The course instructor is also your partner in the class. As always, the more you involve the course instructor in the planning process, the better they can help you.

Divide and Conquer

In addition to the pedagogical advantages of cooperative learning, dividing the class into smaller groups can make things more manageable. The literature lauds the think-pair-share as an ideal cooperative strategy in large classes. Since auditorium seating is usually impossible to move, keep the groups to two or three students so they can communicate effectively.

Put the Students to Work

Many active learning strategies are relatively easy to employ in an auditorium setting. All of the classroom assessment techniques (chapter 6), which serve as active learning strategies, can be used in an auditorium as well as case studies, some games, and role plays. If the students have laptops or other devices connected to the Internet, a structured workshop is also an option.

Check in with the Students

Making a personal connection with the students in a large class can be a challenge—especially in a one-shot setting. One popular and efficient way of checking in with the students is to gather students' input immediately by the use of student response systems or polling (see table 5.1). Before you use any of these, think about what you want to know from the students, when you want to find out, and the best ways to ask; see chapter 6 for specific assessment techniques.

Tip: Use what the course instructor uses in his or her class so the students are familiar and comfortable with the process. You don't want to spend class time teaching students a new technology when there are other ways to assess your class session. Sometimes you can just ask students for a "thumbs up" or "thumbs down" for a yes or no question—no extra equipment required.

TABLE 5.1

A FEW OPTIONS FOR GATHERING INSTANT STUDENT INPUT

Device	Pros	Cons
Clickers/Student Response Systems Clickers resemble remote controls or phones. Each student has his or her own clicker and uses it to respond to a question from the instructor. Responses are sent to the instructor's computer. Results can be displayed (usually in the form of a chart) via software in the instructor's computer (Bruff 2009).	• Can be anonymous • Results can be displayed very easily • If the class uses them all the time, clickers are relatively easy to use • Some clickers allow open-ended questions so you could employ one of Angelo and Cross's classroom assessment techniques (CAT) such as the muddiest point or one-sentence summary (see chapter 6).	• Very expensive (search student response systems in Google for vendors and pricing), but the class instructor might already have clickers.

Device	Pros	Cons
Online Polling Systems The librarian creates an account in a Web-based polling program. Many of these options will work with an electronic device. Some options can be used with regular cell phones and text (SMS) messaging (Sellar 2011).	• Most everyone has a smartphone or related device—and knows how to use it. • You can allow students to use their smartphones in class. • You can ask open-ended questions of students. • The software is easy to set up. • Products are rapidly evolving and offer many options for quick checks for understanding. • Some options are free of charge to teachers.	• You will need software to set up a poll, otherwise you must give your personal number for students to text. • You allow students to use their smartphone in class.
3 x 5 Index Cards (see Case Study in chapter 6)	• Low budget • Low tech • Can be used anywhere • Cards can be reused in other classes	• Limited to binary (yes/no; true/false) or multiple choice questions (unless your eyesight is incredible). • Student responses can be viewed by their peers. • It's more difficult to record results for reflection.

Get Them Out of Their Chairs

The seats in an auditorium may be bolted to the floor, but your students are not bolted to their chairs. There are several learning strategies from chapter 4 that encourage students to get up and moving.

- Gallery walk—If there isn't enough wall space in the auditorium, go out into the hallway

- Fishbowl—Find a few brave volunteers to model. If you can't find a volunteer, you and the course instructor can play the fish. Involve the entire class in the debriefing
- Jigsaw—Jigsaws take some time to plan out, but are a good way to structure small group activities. Karl Smith (2000) recommends giving an assignment or reading to each student in advance and ask them to come to class prepared to share their new expertise with their classmates

With the permission of the instructor, you could send your breakout groups to other more comfortable settings nearby (a lobby, an empty classroom, the great outdoors). If you do this, make sure you assign a timekeeper and give clear instructions about when the group should return to the auditorium.

It is also likely that the auditorium will not have computers; see recommendations below for additional strategies.

In a Classroom with No Computers

Though technology is not a teaching strategy, it is a means to access a lot of the information you and your students will use. Sometimes you will have to teach in a classroom with no computers. If you are presented with this situation in advance, take some time to think about your learning goals and discuss them with the professor. Often your learning goals will be focused on certain information literacy or critical thinking concepts. If this is true, there are many activities that work (and might even work better) without any computers. If you and the instructor really want the students to have hands-on experience practicing certain skills and making use of certain resources that require a computer to use, you should reschedule for a time you can meet in a classroom with computers, or if it is available on your campus, request a laptop cart. Check to see if the course instructor allows or requires students to bring their own laptops (or other electronic devices) to class; if each student has a slightly different device, they can compare their experiences.

Since many classrooms have an instructor's station, you can usually access at least one computer. Even if there is no instructor's station (computers/electronic devices and projectors are very portable nowadays), plan to bring one with you. In the event that you cannot access any computer, you can always bring printed screen captures of what you want the students to analyze and learn about.

Take Advantage of Being Unplugged

There are plenty of strategies for student engagement that do not require a computer. As discussed in chapter 3, due to the time constraints of a one-shot session, librarians often jump ahead to searching and finding before asking students to think critically about certain concepts and brainstorm various parts of the research process. Take the opportunity to develop activities that focus on higher-level thinking.

For example, as mentioned in chapter 3, databases, catalogs, and search engines present all information in a one-dimensional format. Students are left with little context to judge various information sources. Being without computers allows you to demonstrate the structure, content, and context of information by bringing in some three-dimensional examples of various types of information. For example, teach students how to use a book (in print or online) as a research tool, how to differentiate scholarly journals and magazines, how to identify primary and secondary sources, how to read the introductory material of a source, what a citation is, and why professors care so much about using scholarly articles.

Other Student Engagement Strategies That Work Well in a Computer-Free Environment:

- Any strategy that involves writing
- Think-pair-share or interviewing

- Case studies and role play: Print out instructions and any supplementary information in advance. Ask students to think about what kind of information they might need to solve the problem. Then you can explain how to get it.
- Concept maps: Handy for brainstorming
- Jigsaw: Give the students an article or an example of a resource, to look over and teach to others. As mentioned in the section above, Smith (2000) suggests giving the students this assignment in advance so the students are ready to be experts when they arrive in class.

Create various "stations" for students to visit. This works especially well if you host your class in the library. Groups of students can cycle through different areas of the library where you have set up stations designed to allow them to explore different types of information. The use of stations was quite common in the age before computers, and it is still a good strategy today.

Having a few low-tech activities at the ready is always a good idea; there are times when you have planned for a computer classroom, but something goes wrong with the technology (see "Vignette: Teaching in the Dark").

Supplement Your Session

Ideally, your one-shot session is to help students with a certain aspect of a larger project. Bring articles to respond to or examples to discuss. Assign prepwork in advance. As with any other one-shot session, you can point your students to the resources and technology they need with online tutorials, research guides, and so on and thus maximize class time for less technology-focused activities. See chapter 7 for other ideas for supplementing your one-shot.

VIGNETTE: TEACHING IN THE DARK
—Caitlin Bagley, Research and Instruction Librarian,
Murray State University

During my first year as a liaison to the History Department, I got a request for an instruction session for an upper-division course. The professor didn't usually come to the library and didn't bring his students either—so I did my homework. I worked up a detailed presentation, and on the day of the class, I was prepared to go through our collection and JSTOR. I do not rely heavily on paper handouts, and so I was prepared to use a subject guide to show the differences. The class started out fine. There were about fifteen students, for the most part juniors and seniors, who were paying attention. However, horror struck as I clicked over to our databases: the electricity went out.

Suddenly I was faced with a dark classroom, an irritated professor, and fifteen students demanding to be let out early. I spent the first minute or two crossing my fingers and hoping that the power would miraculously come back, but it became increasingly clear that it just wasn't going to happen. I tried to see if I could reschedule with the professor, and he was stubbornly muttering that this was the only time possible, so I ran off to find the building supervisor. The rest of the library was a mess of panicked students who had lost work, and the building supervisor was nowhere to be found so I ran back to my students, and decided that as I had window light, and a white board, I could at least teach them about Boolean operators, and as they were agitated, I was going to do "Simon Says Boolean Operators." If you haven't done this technique before, it's a rather straightforward game where you get students to stand up and represent a search string for you. One way to do this would be to have all students wearing blue jeans stand, then *and* students wearing red caps, and so on until you get down to one or two students standing. The students were game, and as we played the power turned back on to everyone's excitement. I was happy that at least they could take away one thing from the class, even if it was just Boolean searching.

Although you can never fully prepare for the unexpected, I did learn the value of keeping simple activities on hand.

Summary

Your library instruction session may not be in your ideal setting, but there are plenty of strategies to help you succeed in any situation. Remember, the sooner you accept that your class will almost never go exactly as you planned, the better off you will be. The online, auditorium, or no-computer scenarios present challenges, but offer new opportunities as well. As with every class session, it is important to communicate clearly with the course instructor and to be well prepared. Don't fall back on the lecture/demonstration method; there are many ways to keep the students engaged.

"How Will I Know What Worked?"

You have invested time to collaborate with the course instructor, develop your goals, and plan an active and engaging session. But how will you know what worked? The word *assessment* can often inspire dread. One imagines charts, graphs, surveys, focus groups, and complicated statistical software. Too often in education, assessment is the proverbial 800-pound gorilla, which can easily waste institutional and individual time and energy while contributing very little value to teaching and learning. Assessment processes, once in place, may not be revisited for years; and the data that is collected is often not put to any constructive use. Assessment simply for the sake of assessment is not good practice. Often librarians think of assessment as a complicated process, one that is isolated from regular everyday work. In a one-shot environment, this idea can be particularly overwhelming, when time is tight and there's so much to do.

Fortunately, there are practical ways to use your teaching strategies as assessment. No statistical software required! In fact, you may find that you are already incorporating some form of assessment in your one-shot sessions. This chapter invites you to take a fresh look at assessment. It will show you how assessment can be used to improve teaching and learning. A number of practical assessment strategies are described, which can be implemented by individual teacher librarians and do not require institutional resources. Finally, it offers suggestions on how to use assessment to improve your teaching.

Assessment takes place on different levels: classroom, program, and institution. This chapter will focus on assessment at the classroom level, because teaching librarians have control and influence over the classroom, but may not have that authority at the programmatic or institutional level. Classroom assessment is well suited to one-shot library instruction because such instruction is course-based, so it makes sense to assess it on the classroom level. For a more comprehensive look at assessment of information literacy programs, please see the list of related information literacy assessment resources.

RELATED INFORMATION LITERACY ASSESSMENT RESOURCES

Booth, Char. 2011. *Reflective Teaching, Effective Learning: Instructional Literacy for Library Educators.* Chicago: American Library Association.

Gilchrist, Debra, and Anne Zald. 2008. "Instruction and Program Design Through Assessment." In *Information Literacy Instruction Handbook,* ed. C. Cox and E. Lindsay. Chicago: Association of College and Research Libraries.

Mackey, T., and T. Jacobson. 2010. *Collaborative Information Literacy Assessments: Strategies for Evaluating Teaching and Learning.* New York: Neal-Schuman.

Oakleaf, M. 2008. "Dangers and Opportunities: A Conceptual Map of Information Literacy Assessment Approaches." *Portal: Libraries and the Academy* 8, no. 3: 233—53.

Oakleaf, M., and N. Kaske. 2009. "Guiding Questions for Assessing Information Literacy in Higher Education." *Portal: Libraries and the Academy* 9, no. 2: 273—86.

Radcliff, Carolyn J. et al. 2007. *A Practical Guide to Information Literacy Assessment for Academic Librarians*. Westport, CT: Libraries Unlimited.

Wilkinson, Carroll, and Courtney Bruch, eds. 2012. *Transforming Information Literacy Programs: Intersecting Frontiers of Self, Library Culture, and Campus Community*. Chicago: Association of College and Research Libraries.

Why Bother with Assessment?

Assessment is a formidable challenge in a one-shot environment. After all, time and access to students is limited. You might assume that taking time to assess will detract from student learning, but in fact, the opposite is true. Classroom assessment invites students to become active participants in their own learning and eventually empowers them to become more critical, self-directed learners. Paradoxically, with so little time spent with students in an instructional setting (often less than an hour in a semester-long course), one-shot library instructors have *more* reason to incorporate assessment rather than less. Booth states the situation: "The rationale for focusing on assessment in library instruction is simple: because of our limited learning interactions, it is important to open as many windows of evaluation as possible to determine if actionable insight is being built" (2011, 138).

Classroom assessment can easily be reasonably and seamlessly integrated into one-shot library instruction (Angelo and Cross 1993; Radcliff et al. 2007). Classroom assessment is formative, meaning that its goal is to improve teaching and learning. In a one-shot library instruction environment, classroom assessment is the most manageable form of assessment because it does not require a lot of resources. It requires little time, little or no money, and does not require a lot of expertise (meaning it's really hard to screw it up). When done well, classroom assessment is driven by programmatic and institutional goals related to student success. It can produce bountiful data that can be analyzed and shared in order to start conversations that ultimately have programmatic and institutional impact (for examples, see Long and Shrikhande 2010; Zald and Millet 2012).

Many teaching librarians work in isolation. On the practical side, classroom assessment is attractive because of the ease with which an individual teaching librarian, acting alone, can implement it. On the hopeful side, classroom assessment can and should lead to increased collaboration with institutional partners. So, for example, if your classroom assessment uncovers gaps in student learning, a conversation with teaching faculty might occur that leads to changes in the assignment, additional information literacy instruction, or instructional follow-up in class. In the best-case scenario, quality classroom assessment can lead to scholarly publication and presentations, teaching awards, and overall greater understanding and recognition of your information literacy program's vital role in the larger educational program.

One Librarian, One-Shot: How to Assess with Limited Resources

You may already be engaged in some basic informal assessment practices. Every time you ask students questions, observe students performing research, or think critically about how an information literacy session went, if you use that knowledge to make positive changes to instruction, you are informally assessing teaching and learning. Fortunately, the intelligence, curiosity, and good pedagogy that inform quality teaching also inform quality classroom assessment. Rather than being mutually exclusive, teaching and assessing should be naturally intertwined. When teaching and assessing are integrated, your teaching and learning will improve (Segers, Dochy, and Gijbels 2010). It's important to tie your assessment to your learning goals—the facts, skills, concepts, and attitudes that you have prioritized while planning your session. Assessment experts such as Gilchrist and Zald (2008) use formally articulated learning outcomes, à la Bloom's taxonomy. The advantage to this method is to write your goals (learning objectives) as verbs, making them easier to observe. For example, the student will learn to apply Boolean search terms in *Academic Search Premier* in order to focus their search for articles. Chapter

3 recommends that you avoid spending too much time on the structure and wording of these goals, but to use your goals to focus and prioritize your planning for the class. Ideally, your teaching strategies will be tied to your goals, thus creating a natural setting for your assessment.

Despite the many limitations of a one-shot session and the pervasive phenomenon of scarce resources, it is possible for you to easily take your existing classroom practices and turn them into more formal classroom assessment. Using simple engaging learning activities, you can begin to document students' thoughts, feelings, and actions (cognition, affect, and behavior). That documentation in turn will provide data that will help you improve your teaching, whether in the moment or in future sessions. A simple, low-tech approach is often best; Gilchrist and Zald summed it up beautifully with their statement, "You can do a lot with five minutes and a 3 × 5 card" (2008, 173).

Assessment can seem overwhelming to individual one-shot library instructors because traditionally assessment is thought of as summative, statistical, and complicated. It is refreshing to consider that there are many useful assessments that have none of those unpleasant qualities, are fun for both instructors and students, and best of all, improve student understanding of information literacy. Following are some of the types of classroom assessment that are discussed in the literature.

Doing It with Class: Classroom Assessment Techniques

Angelo and Cross coined the term *classroom assessment techniques* and provide detailed descriptions of fifty techniques (1993). Many of the techniques have been adapted to assess one-shot information literacy instruction. Among the most popular are:

- The *one-minute paper*, described in chapter 4.
- The *muddiest point*, an adaptation of the one-minute paper that poses the question "What was the muddiest (least clear) point in today's session?" In a one-shot session, you may want to do this midway through your class.

- The *one-sentence summary,* which prompts students to summarize their understanding of an information literacy concept in one sentence.
- *Directed paraphrasing,* which challenges students to express complex information literacy concepts in simple language for a specific audience. (For example, see the "Vignette" in chapter 4.)
- *Applications cards,* which are useful after students have learned a broad concept. The instructor passes out a card that prompts the students to explain the concept in the context of a real-world situation. These could be used for the threshold concepts discussed in chapter 3; a prompt could be: "Describe an instance when you were asked to pay for information" (most students will have paid for a music or movie download, bought a magazine or book, etc.).
- *Defining features matrix,* which requires students to distinguish features between closely related concepts or resources, such as two similar databases or popular magazines, professional, and scholarly publications.

VIGNETTE: WHO NEEDS HIGH-TECH?
—Jason Snyder, Librarian for Online Services and liaison librarian for the English Department
—Nancy Frazier, Instructional Services Librarian and liaison librarian for the History Department, Bucknell University

Making the most of a fifty-minute class session is nothing new. This particular session—an information literacy instruction session for a large group for an English class (ENGL 199—Survey of British and American Literature) led us to some creative problem-solving. The course is made up of three sections, which meet independently with three different English professors, and one common hour, in which all three sections meet together to hear guest lecturers and engage in other large-group activities. It was this common hour in which our session was held.

Jason: I've had excellent rapport with the English Department during my tenure at Bucknell. I was an undergraduate here, so I've known many of the faculty for most of my professional life. They are always my "best customers" in terms of user education and liaison work. During this session, I like to showcase faculty scholarship and their activities outside the classroom, so that students get a fuller picture of what their professors do. I typically have the three ENGL 199 professors talk about their scholarship, what research means to their careers and tenure/promotion, and then I pass around books and articles they've published to show students examples of their scholarly work.

Nancy: We've had great results using a simple classroom assessment technique for the combined session for the ENGL 199 class of approximately seventy-five students. Initially, we explored using clickers or students' phones, but we wanted to maximize instructional time with a free and easy way to involve students and gauge their understanding. In the past, I'd seen a simple classroom assessment technique used effectively with a Bucknell physics class. The professor gave each student a set of index cards numbered 1 to 5, and posted questions with corresponding numbered responses. The professor was able to quickly assess comprehension and make adjustments in delivery of content.

We adapted this method for the large group by distributing three brightly colored index cards to each student. Throughout the fifty-minute session, we posed questions (via PowerPoint slides) with corresponding color-coded responses. Students simply held up the card that matched the color-coded response they chose. The professors were able to scan the room to get a feel for what students know. Benefits include being able to adapt to student needs on the fly, tailor explanations based on student responses, and give students the chance to participate and ask questions. The casual, conversational tone we used with the students, with each other, and with the faculty made the class more interactive, and minimized the limitations of teaching a large class in a large auditorium.

Jason: Faculty involved later told me that they enjoyed the opportunity to discuss their scholarship with undergraduate students. The following semester, the professors teaching ENGL 199 asked if Nancy and I could "do the same thing as last semester," so I take that as positive reinforcement of a job well done!

Classroom assessment techniques are well suited to one-shot library instruction because they are integrated into teaching and learning and do not require expertise to design and use. They are the very activities you need to engage your students and help you accomplish your goals. They are versatile and can be used to assess students' thoughts, feelings, and actions (cognition, affect, and behavior). Most importantly, they engage students and improve student understanding of complex information literacy concepts and processes.

Classroom assessment techniques are often used at the end of classes in order to investigate what the students have learned and to uncover future teaching and learning opportunities. But the real beauty of these techniques is that they can be used at any point during the one-shot session because they are also serving as active learning strategies. At the beginning of the session they immediately engage the learner, set the tone for an interactive session, and can drive the class agenda. They can be used at any point during library instruction when you notice that students are confused or not paying attention, or they can be used at the end of class for wrap-up and debriefing. At whatever point you decide to use them, one of the greatest benefits is that by asking for student input and encouraging students to take responsibility for their learning, you demonstrate that you value them as learners.

How you implement these techniques is also flexible. If you are short on time, you might simply distribute 3 × 5 cards and collect them for later analysis. Better practice, if possible, is to have some small group or whole class debriefing, or both. Whenever students are engaged in a self- or peer-directed activity, you have an opportunity to further assess using the simple tool of observation. You should circulate the room watching and listening to the students. Often you will spot students who are struggling and will have the opportunity to differentiate your information literacy instruction by intervening and redirecting the student, or following up later. To formalize the assessment aspect of the process, you can jot down notes which later can form the basis of a reflective narrative in a teaching journal.

You will grow more comfortable with these techniques with experience. It's best to begin casually and build up to more formal use of classroom assessment techniques to gather data. Some information literacy instructors are using more advanced technology in their classroom assessment. For example, online polling or word cloud software can be used to collect real-time student input instead of 3 × 5 cards. For an example of the use of word cloud software and the one-minute paper to assess the impact of library instruction on student attitudes, see figure 6.1.

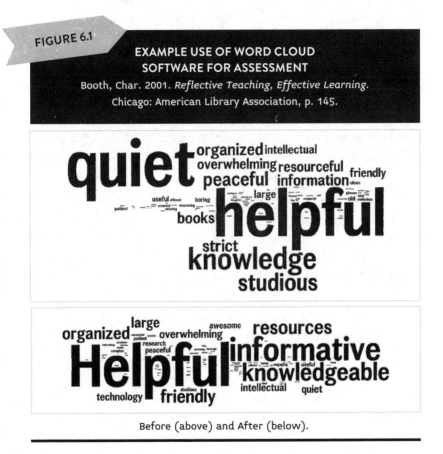

FIGURE 6.1

EXAMPLE USE OF WORD CLOUD SOFTWARE FOR ASSESSMENT

Booth, Char. 2001. *Reflective Teaching, Effective Learning.* Chicago: American Library Association, p. 145.

Before (above) and After (below).

Take It up a Notch with Performance Assessments

As you become more comfortable with informal classroom assessment, you may choose to enter the ambitious world of performance assessment.

Simply put, a performance assessment occurs when you evaluate how well a student completes a specific task. You can use a final product, such as an annotated bibliography or a term paper; or you might evaluate a process through observation. In a one-shot session, it may be simpler to focus on a process.

One very simple example of documenting a process is to have students write down the steps for finding an article; their methods may vary, allowing you to observe the information-seeking behavior of different students. A more elaborate approach would be to ask students to create their own research guide or handout. Instead of giving them a handout with instructions and resources, have them develop their own guide during class. This allows the students to apply what they are learning in class to their individual needs. In order to document the process, you can ask the students to create their guides on a computer/device and e-mail you a copy, or have them post the guides online in Google Drive or on a wiki. Another option would be (with permission from the students and the course instructor) to collect the paper handouts, add comments and suggestions, and return them to the professor for the next class period. You can evaluate the products outside of class or also, if time allows, the teaching librarian, students, and classroom instructor can evaluate them as a group during the debriefing session.

Performance assessment of a product is more commonly conducted outside of class time, such as in collaboration with the classroom instructor on grading papers or projects.

Common examples of how performance assessment is used by teacher librarians include analyses of student bibliographies, writing, or portfolios. This approach requires a significant amount of collaboration, planning, time, and expertise, but it is attainable. The trickiest part is developing a performance-based assessment tool that is aligned with the goals of the course for which one-shot instruction is being conducted, measures what it is supposed to measure (is valid), and measures those criteria consistently (is reliable).

One of the best ways to assess student performance is to use a rubric to accompany research assignments. Popham writes that "a rubric is little more than a scoring guide with a fancy name" (2010, 119). While there are a growing number of examples in the literature of the use of rubrics to assess information literacy independently (for example, Diller and Phelps, 2008), one-shot library instructors are more likely to contribute one or two information literacy-related criteria to a rubric which is designed in collaboration with the classroom instructor for holistic evaluation of a student paper or project (for example, Gasper and Presser, 2010). Rubrics also contain levels of quality, which can be labeled or numbered. Typically the evaluative criteria and levels of quality are arranged in a grid. See table 6.1 for an example criterion and levels of quality that could be included in a rubric.

TABLE 6.1

EXAMPLE OF INFORMATION LITERACY CRITERION AND LEVELS OF QUALITY FOR A RUBRIC

Objective: Students will use a range of sources sufficient to answer research questions (e.g., books, journal articles, reports, primary sources, etc.)

Levels of Quality			
Not Acceptable	**Needs Improvement**	**Meets Expectations**	**Exceptional**
Did not include a bibliography	Needed a greater range of sources to answer research questions	Used an adequate range of sources to answer research questions	Used an exemplary range of resources to answer research questions

Despite this simple example, constructing quality rubrics is not a simple task. It requires knowledge and skill. For more information about how to construct rubrics, consult your campus teaching center, Radcliff et al.'s chapter on performance assessment in *A Practical Guide to Information Literacy Assessment for Academic Librarians* (2007), or one of the many professional teaching books that explain how to develop rubrics.

An investment of your time and energy to create rubrics will:

- Make your expectations clear for students, so that they are better able to meet them
- Provide the basis for collaboration and conversation with teaching faculty
- Measure the higher-order thinking skills that are necessary to demonstrate information literacy
- Provide concrete data that can establish the impact of information literacy instruction to institutional partners and the wider public

What About Tests, Quizzes, and Surveys?

Tests, in the common multiple choice or true-false format, are not the best option for one-shot sessions for a number of reasons: most multiple choice and true/false type tests are suitable for assessing lower-level thinking skills and basic recall of facts, so they are unlikely to shed much light on the complex process of student information literacy. It also requires expertise to create tests that measure what they are supposed to measure (are valid) and measure it consistently (are reliable). Most teaching librarians do not possess this expertise, even though most information literacy tests are librarian-created. Finally, even the very word *test* takes away from the positive, supportive environment that librarians want to create. Quizzes and mini-tests, administered on the fly, and used to check for understanding, are more suited to the one-shot session than more formal measurement. In a one-shot session, quizzes and surveys should be similar to the one-minute paper and other classroom assessment techniques. They should be brief, student-centered, and low risk.

Like tests, most quizzes are better for assessing a student's knowledge of basic facts. A quiz can be handy if you want to make sure the students have gathered some critical, basic information before you move on to more difficult concepts. For example, you may want to use a quiz to check student understanding of plagiarism. Keep the quiz to a few questions. Open-ended questions are often more effective than multiple choice as a way of assessing understanding; they allow you to witness some of the thought process behind the answers. Most of the classroom assessment techniques discussed above can be used as a short quiz (as a check for understanding) in place of a more traditional multiple-choice version. If you are checking in with students as you teach, you will not be able to grade the papers in a matter of moments. Instead, go over the answers as a group and ask students to think about their own responses. If you collect the quizzes at the end of the class, you can use them to inform your future sessions with other classes. You can also use the student response options described in the table in chapter 5 for a quick quiz.

Surveys can be used to gauge students' thoughts and feelings about a class. Keep any surveys to one or two questions and focus on what you really want to know (did they think the class was relevant to their research project? Did they think the activities were a good use of class time?). Lengthy surveys can often be confusing and poorly constructed. There is no need for an elaborate survey to assess a one-shot session. You can pose a few questions quickly at the end of class via an online form or a piece of paper. Keep the survey anonymous if you want honest feedback! In-class surveys are your best guarantee for good response rates, but depending on your questions, you may want to survey the students later in the semester, after they have completed their research project. Surveys might also be used before a one-shot session to gauge student expectations for the class or assess their needs. Ask the instructor to distribute the survey. For instance, "what is the one thing you want to be able to do at the end of your session?" In this example, a one-minute paper can serve as a "survey."

Follow Up with a Post-Instruction Interview

Ideally, your communication with the instructor should continue even
after the one-shot session is over. Remember that in a one-shot session,
you may be able to see if the students are "getting it," but the course
instructor will be the witness to the synthesis and application of the
information. Following up with the instructor can be difficult; you both
have demands on your time and it is easy just to move on to the next
class after the session is over. Following up can be as simple as a quick
phone call, or sending a short survey. A survey is convenient because
you can send the same (or similar) questions to multiple instructors,
but response rates may vary. Whether it is a phone call, face-to-face,
or a survey, use this post-instruction interview to ask questions about
how helpful the session was, what might be done differently the next
time, and so on. You probably won't have time to have a meaningful
conversation with each instructor you work with, so start with a few
each semester. These conversations are worthy of your time because
they will improve your future one-shot sessions—and they often lead
to a more integrated or strategic model of library instruction.

to evaluate your instructional style (listed in order from least to most time-consuming):

> Do your own one-minute paper at the end of class while the students are doing theirs. Your self-imposed prompt could be: What's one thing I will do differently next time? *Or* what's one thing that really worked well in this session?
>
> Attend a colleague's class and participate as if you were a student. Afterward, write down your impressions: What did you enjoy in the student's role? What didn't work as well for you?
>
> Ask a colleague to attend your class. Develop a few essential questions about what you want to know. Center your questions on your learning goals. Here is your chance to get input from another information literacy expert.
>
> With permission from the students and instructor, record your class session and watch it twice. The first time, watch yourself—it's hard not to! Don't be overly critical about your idiosyncrasies; focus on the characteristics that Filene (2005) says all good teachers share: "enthusiasm . . . clarity . . . organization" and the desire for their students to succeed (7). The next time, however, watch the students. Are they engaged? Do they seem to be following what you say or are they confused? Observe the video as if you are evaluating a colleague, and be easy on yourself.
>
> Join (or start) a group. The terminology varies (teaching circles, communities of practice, professional learning communities), but many schools and campuses have some sort of group where professionals share their experiences.
>
> Pay attention. Librarians are experts at gathering information from a variety of sources. Look for information and inspiration in everyday life such as professional literature, blogs, conferences, and casual conversations. Char Booth calls this practice of gathering wisdom from what we see, experience, hear, and read "gleaning" (2011, 26). Good teachers are continuous learners.

What Do I Do with the Data?

As mentioned throughout this chapter, the purpose of assessing one-shot instruction is to empower teaching librarians to improve student learning. It is not enough to simply collect student data. You must also reflect on the data and take action. In this context, assessment is a continuous and cyclical process that Booth describes as reflect, revise, reuse (2011). If possible, take time after the session to critically reflect on what worked and what could be better. Just as you have been encouraged to take risks with your teaching throughout this book, you must be willing to self-evaluate and change. As Gilchrist and Zald remind us: "excellence does not require perfection" (2008, 186).

Critical self-reflection is a powerful habit of mind for teachers to develop. If you formalize the process by keeping a log or reflection journal, you will be able to refer back to it in the future. If you don't like to journal, add some notes to your calendar. One-shot library instruction usually occurs for the same courses each semester, so such a record is invaluable when it comes time to teach that particular course again.

It is also important to share your data. Sharing with the students in the class through discussion will promote student engagement with information literacy concepts and help the students to critically reflect. Sharing with the course instructor will promote collaboration and instructional improvement. Sharing with other librarians formally and informally is a service to the profession. And sharing with other campus communities will strengthen your information literacy program.

The formalization of the process of assessing, reflecting, revising, and sharing can be a form of scholarship that is known as action research in the K–12 world and the Scholarship of Teaching and Learning (SoTL) across colleges and universities. Whether or not you are required to produce scholarship by your institution, sharing your experiences through conference presentations and publication is an outstanding professional development activity. For an excellent example of how a simple classroom assessment technique can be developed into a scholarly research article, see Choinski and Emanuel (2006).

Summary

In order to tackle assessment in a one-shot session, you will have to stop thinking of assessment as an additional demand on your time. While much assessment is poorly designed and ineffectually used, it is possible for individual librarians to conduct assessment on the classroom level that can richly inform teaching and learning. Effective assessment has immediate positive impact on teaching and learning and can have demonstrable impact on program and institutional goals over time.

Asking questions, observing students, and reflecting on your teaching are informal assessment techniques. These aspects of teaching can be formalized and used as data collection tools through the use of classroom assessment techniques (Angelo and Cross, 1993). Classroom assessment techniques are suitable for one-shot instruction because of their flexibility and adaptability and can be used as your active learning techniques for your session. Performance assessments can also be useful for assessing the process during a session or a product after the session. Rubrics are a robust tool to assess performance. Quizzes and surveys can be effective ways to check for student understanding or to gauge students' opinions about the class session. Reflection is an important part of the assessment cycle, and data becomes meaningful when it is reflected upon and used to make positive changes to instruction. Assessment is a continuous and cyclical process. It is also important to share your reflections and ideas with students, teaching faculty, other librarians, and other campus communities. For those librarians with responsibilities for producing scholarship and those interested in developing professionally, one outcome of assessment can be presentable, publishable scholarship in the form of action research or SoTL.

"There's Not Enough of Me to Go Around!"
What to Do When You Become a Victim of Your Own Success

Well, now you've done it. You've formed solid collaborations with course instructors and planned and implemented engaging, effective classes. Instruction requests are flying in as more and more course instructors ask you to come to their classes. Congratulations on your success! Take a moment to pat yourself on the back, and then take a deep breath, because there is still more to do if you are to sustain your teaching practice. Obviously a one-shot does not an information-literate person make. You are barely scratching the surface with just a one-shot session—there's so much more you could teach. And, oh yeah, you have all these other responsibilities (reference, collection development, etc.).

So what can you do once you become a victim of your own success? This chapter will help you reflect on your progress, prioritize your duties, manage your time, supplement your one-shot session, and develop a more strategic approach to your information literacy program.

But first, let's review some basic truths:

1. You are just one person.
2. There are only so many hours in a day.
3. No one becomes information literate after one class session (or even after a course or many courses).
4. You are not solely responsible for students' information literacy.

Get Your Bearings
Reflect

Chapter 6 encourages you to reflect after each class session (if at all possible), but you should also reflect on an entire semester or year in order to better understand how you are spending your time (and why you're feeling so overwhelmed). Semester breaks are usually a good time to reflect on the previous semester, since it is a relatively slow time for academic libraries. Begin by listing the classes you taught that semester. Reflect on the time spent working with course instructors and planning your class session. If you kept a journal, collected various student or faculty assessments (see chapter 6), or have a stack of handouts and notes, look through them and contemplate what worked and what you will do differently in the future. If your instruction was to support a semester-long project, call the course instructor to see how the projects turned out (they may let you see the final products). Now that you have thought about the semester as a whole, ask yourself a series of critical questions:

- Which were the most important/effective class sessions?
- Were there class sessions where one session was not enough?
- Did the students know why they were there?

- Did you see lots of the same students again and again in multiple sessions?
- Were there activities that took you hours to prepare, and if so, were they worth it? Can you adapt them for other classes?
- Are there other activities that would emphasize the same skills and concepts, with less preparation?

The answers to these questions will help you find gaps and redundancies in your offerings, and think about your time investment for each class.

Strategize (and Prioritize)

Another good way to reflect on your last semester or year is to look at the classes you have conducted as they relate to the college curriculum. This process is a one-shot version of curriculum mapping, which is usually more elaborate and program-wide, but with the same intent—checking to see if your intended outcomes match up with what you are actually teaching (English 2006). There are software options for doing this that might be especially useful if your information literacy program collects and analyzes statistics that can be captured digitally. Or you can keep it simple and just make a table (see table 7.1).

The table should provide perspective on how you are spending your time and intellectual energy. What stands out? In this example, a good deal of this librarian's time is instructing first-year students. Academic libraries commonly emphasize introductions to information literacy in the first year where it is a natural fit as an introduction to college life. The peril is that instructors may assume that once the students have had that introduction, they don't need any additional information literacy sessions. This assumption is as faulty as thinking that one yoga class gives you balance and flexibility for the rest of your life. Students need information literacy instruction throughout their college careers to exercise and reinforce the basic concepts they have learned as well as to develop skills specific to their majors.

TABLE 7.1

EXAMPLE OF A SIMPLE TABLE OF CLASSES TAUGHT AND RELATIONSHIP TO THE COLLEGE CURRICULUM

First Year	Sophomore/ Junior Years	Senior	Graduate	Other
12 ENG 101 classes 3 first-year seminars 7 study skills classes		Capstone class for nursing students	Research methods class for physical therapy students	2 tours for the local elementary school, international students, and new faculty

Try this. Pick one program or major, read through the course catalog, and write down the courses that all majors are required to take. Then choose the ones where information literacy and research skills are most needed (or required) for the course; talk to a faculty member or two in the department to confirm your choices. The resulting table might look like table 7.2.

TABLE 7.2

EXAMPLE OF A SIMPLE TABLE OF CLASSES THAT ALL STUDENTS TAKE AND WHICH BENEFIT FROM INFORMATION LITERACY INSTRUCTION

First Year	Second Year	Senior	Graduate
ENG 101 classes	Introduction to the major research methods	Capstone	Research methods

Tip: You get extra points if you go through this exercise with multiple members (and leaders) of the program's academic department.

This chart is more sparse (and balanced) than the previous one. These are your core courses; the ones to reach out to every year, the ones most likely expand into more than just one-shot per semester, and the ones where you are most likely to have a lasting impact. Everything else is extra. Everything else builds on this core. That doesn't mean you shouldn't work with any other classes, but core courses should take priority when you start getting requests next semester.

"NO"—YOUR BIGGEST TIME SAVER

Sure, it's easy to sit in your office and decide your priorities or discuss program-level priorities with your colleagues, but then the course instructor calls and asks for your help. A lot of librarians agree to teaching any one-shot "to get a foot in the door" and show the course instructor what they can do. That's really not a good enough reason to provide a one-shot session; in fact, agreeing to teach a library session when there is no concrete point of need sets a problematic precedent for the future. You don't have to just say yes or no. Go back to the reference interview model from chapter 2—librarians don't answer a reference question with a yes or a no; rather, they ask more clarifying questions and explain their responses. If the answer is no, librarians provide reasonable alternatives. The same goes for a one-shot session. Some of the supplements and alternatives to the face-to-face session that are listed in this chapter are good compromises to offer if you say no.

In addition to course curricula, take a look at the priorities of your library and institution. Almost all libraries have some sort of statement about information literacy in their mission or goals, and most colleges have some sort of institutional expectation of information literacy concepts, in a strategic plan, general education program, or institutional mission, even if they don't use the precise phrase "information literacy." In 2010, 32.7 percent of academic libraries reported that information literacy was incorporated into their institution's mission (U.S. Department of Education's National Center for Education Statistics, 2011). All of the U.S. regional accrediting agencies emphasize expectations for information literacy skills (Saunders 2007). Take a look at the criteria that apply to your institution.

Some libraries will have very detailed information literacy plans (as recommended by ACRL), while others are more broad, vague, or exist only in the minds of each librarian. If you have a detailed plan or clearly outlined library and institutional expectations, see how they are matching up with what you are actually doing. If your library or institution does not have such goals, it's time for some strategic planning.

When you reflect upon your semester, also take a look at *all* of your responsibilities, not just your teaching duties. Make a list of the things that are actually part of your job description, things that you do as part of a service or scholarship requirement, and the things that you volunteered to do. As you look at this very long list, think about the following:

- Is this activity the best use of my time?
- Does it match up with the departmental/library/ institutional mission?
- Who can help me with this? Is it possible to delegate this to someone else?
- Is there a more efficient process for this task?

You will find things you can drop, delegate, or streamline (if you don't, you may be feeling too subjective about the process and should ask someone else to help you). If you are struggling, pick up a guide to time management that can help you. Also, keep your boss in the loop in this decision-making process, especially when dropping tasks or delegating to others.

TIME MANAGEMENT BOOKS

You are not alone! There are time management books made just for librarians. Here are two good choices:

McKnight, Michelynn. 2010. *The Agile Librarian's Guide to Thriving in Any Institution*. Santa Barbara, CA: Libraries Unlimited.
Siess, Judith A. 2002. *Time Management, Planning, and Prioritization for Librarians*. Lanham, MD: Scarecrow.

Get Help

Librarians are superheroes, but they aren't superhuman. If you see that help is needed to keep your information literacy program flourishing, it is okay to ask for it. Using your reflection as a guide, try to pinpoint where help is needed and what kinds of support are needed. Chances are there are things that someone else can do (possibly even better). Think about how to articulate what you need from others and approach people, such as your supervisor, with possible solutions. Don't expect easy solutions. Brainstorming and negotiation are part of the process. Sometimes, the solutions will involve financial or staff resources, so do some homework in advance. For example, you may realize that you could design your research guides in less time with ready-made software designed for that purpose; or your collection development efforts might be streamlined by an approval plan. Other solutions may be more accessible or affordable. You may have a colleague, a student worker, intern, or other staff member who can help you with your teaching load or with other aspects of your job. Many librarians, out of a desire to help, regularly perform clerical tasks that would be better suited to other staff. These types of tasks should be the first to go.

Approach all stakeholders with possible solutions rather than with problems. "I think this might work better if . . ." or "How do you think this might work better?" will be more effective than "This isn't working."

Make sure you are having real two-way conversations with people rather than complaining or telling them what to do.

Who Can Help with the One-Shot? Your Coworkers

In addition to delegating or sharing duties with others, take a team approach to planning and evaluating class sessions. Create a place to share teaching activities, tutorials, and so on. As mentioned in chapter 6, a professional learning community is a good way to talk about experiences, explore solutions, and get new ideas from colleagues. Talk to colleagues in informal settings too. Even if you devote several hours a month to sharing and discussion, the resulting intellectual and moral support from your peers can make the exact same course load seem easier.

Your Boss

If you are feeling overburdened or want to change your instruction program, your boss may be able to help you manage your workload, delegate to others, or change the library's approach to instruction. If you are not comfortable approaching your supervisor on a regular basis, work the conversation into your performance review. McKnight (2010) offers suggestions for educating your boss:

- Do not lecture, insult their intelligence, or overwhelm them with literature on the topic.
- Find out what they already know: "The boss may understand more than you think; subtly ask open-ended questions in context" (69).
- Introduce "complex concepts" (like a new approach to your information literacy program) in small bits over time (69). According to McKnight, it's a mark of success if your boss ends up presenting these ideas as his or her own.

Faculty

Ideally, information literacy is reinforced throughout the semester by the course instructor—good communication and planning with the instructor will help. Say no when a one-shot doesn't makes sense. Provide supplementary support if you aren't available to (or aren't asked to) teach additional sessions for a course. Broader conversations with academic departments can help you identify the best times and places to offer instruction and help you avoid scattershot delivery.

Supplement or Provide Alternatives to the Face-to-Face Session

The following are methods for stretching the one-shot beyond the fifty- to 120-minute class session, or in some cases replacing it altogether. Many are handy in online classes too. Some of these methods can also be presented as an alternative to a face-to-face one-shot.

Before Class
Assign Homework—to the Course Instructor

Remember that the course instructor is a partner in information literacy. At the very least you want to make sure the instructor has explained the expectations for the assignment. There are other things the course instructor can do for you. For example, you could also ask the instructor to talk about what research is like in his or her field, have the students practice reading and summarizing a scholarly journal article, or brainstorm topics in class. You can also ask the instructor to form groups in advance to save time in your one-shot session.

"Flip" Your Class (Bergmann and Sams, 2012)

In a flipped classroom, students are asked to watch a video (or use some other instructional tool) the night before class. The content focuses on what would normally be taught during class time. When the class meets, the instructor reviews the video and then the students spend most of the class session working independently on a project/activity (what would normally be done as homework) while the instructor provides guidance.

Guided practice is already a good part of a library workshop, but to flip your class, you will provide some information in advance. Bergmann and Sams focus mainly on videos, but encourage instructors to ask themselves: "Which activities that do not require my physical presence can be shifted out of the class in order to give more class time to activities that are enhanced by my presence?" (96). The answer to that question will be the "homework" you ask the course instructor to assign to the students before they come to class. This could be a video, a tutorial, a short slide show, or an exercise. Keep your videos short. If you don't have time to create your own video or tutorial, use an existing video—ACRL's PRIMO database and MERLOT have a variety of peer-reviewed learning objects.

After Class
Use Online Research Guides

Since you are ditching the demo in a one-shot session, save the "go here, click there" information for a research guide. Give the students the URL for the guide and ask the instructor to add it to the syllabus/learning management system.

Use the Online Learning Management System

Distance courses and many face-to-face courses have some sort of online learning management system (LMS). This is a good way to communicate with the students both before and after the class session. Wikis, blogs, and discussion boards can be used to answer frequently asked questions for the whole class or clear up muddy points from the one-shot session.

Consider Tutorials

Tutorials are handy for the flipped classroom model above, but they are also great as a follow-up. For example, if your classroom assessment uncovered that a few concepts were still not clear, provide a simple tutorial for the instructor to show in a later class, embed into an LMS, or add it to an existing research guide. Tutorials don't have to be fancy.

Leverage Existing Services

Your library likely already provides many point-of-need services where your students can follow up for more information and help: research assistance services in person, by phone, chat/e-mail/SMS, and individual appointments. Some librarians are disappointed when a student from a class follows up for more information—they feel they have failed in some way, but the contrary is true. A goal for most information literacy sessions is that students see the library and librarians as an important partner in their academic success. These services allow you to provide one-on-one assistance to the students who need more help.

Ask for Additional Time with the Students

Teaching several sessions throughout the semester is another way to supplement your one-shot and will help you reach students throughout the stages of their research. Be strategic in this approach. This is a good strategy for the core courses you identified earlier in this chapter.

Fly-by the Classroom

A fly-by is a five- to fifteen-minute drop-in session with a class to introduce yourself, a quick concept, or a resource such as a research guide. Fly-by sessions are an option if:

- The course instructor really wants you to work with his or her class but does not have a specific research assignment. Instead of scheduling a full session, pop into the class, introduce yourself, point out your research guides, and so on, so students know how to get help when they need it.

- The students have an explicit information need, but the course professor is reluctant to give up a whole class session.
- Following the one-shot session, you and the course instructor agree that brief follow-up is necessary or desirable.

In any case, be honest with the instructor and yourself about what can be accomplished in a five- to ten-minute visit. Fly-bys are not meant to replace what you can do in a full fifty- to sixty-minute presentation for a class that really needs one, but they can be useful when used strategically.

Next Steps

Probably the worst aspect of only getting one shot with a class is realizing how much more the students could learn if you had more time. There are many different ways to go beyond the one-shot session; the model you choose for your library will depend on a number of factors such as the culture of your institution, your library, faculty buy-in, and what is realistic to accomplish based on staffing and other priorities.

Going beyond the one-shot can be as simple as offering some of the supplementary strategies listed in this chapter or as elaborate as programs that offer for-credit courses and "embedded librarians." ACRL offers *Characteristics of Programs of Information Literacy that Illustrate Best Practices: A Guideline* (2012) as guidance when designing, refining, or expanding an information literacy program (warning: this is not meant to be a checklist, but rather a compilation of best practices across libraries). The characteristics include many things that you are already doing, such as collaborating and using good pedagogy.

Two ways to build upon the individual instruction that you already offer are the curriculum-integrated model and the embedded librarian model.

The Curriculum-Integrated Model

In this scenario:

> [The information literacy curriculum is] campuswide;
> problem-based, inquiry-based, and resource-based (that is,
> it uses a variety of information resources); makes effec-
> tive use of instructional pedagogies and technologies; is
> learner-centered; and is integrated and articulated with a
> discipline's learning outcomes. It enhances and expands
> student learning through a coherent, systematic approach
> that facilitates the transfer of learning across the curricu-
> lum. (Rockman 2004, 16)

This description highlights many of the qualities that this book has encouraged you to include in a one-shot session, including active, student-centered learning and a connection to the learning outcomes of the course. The key differences are the inclusion of the terms "campuswide," "articulation," "systematic approach," and "across the curriculum." Ideally, in this model, students would build on certain information literacy skills and concepts in specific courses throughout their college careers. Course instructors and librarians could have basic expectations for the students as they progress; for example, a sophomore has been introduced to certain aspects of source evaluation and can find and identify a scholarly journal article in the field of chemistry or use resources to describe the physical properties of a certain chemical.

Many proponents of the curriculum integration model encourage librarians to work with high levels of administration to ensure that information literacy skills are written into mission statements, strategic plans, general education curricula, and so on, but you can also start small. An exercise like the one in table 7.2 is a way of articulating specific courses in the curriculum. If you do this exercise, or something similar, with an academic department, you are establishing a more systematic approach, and with the right levels of support, it can gradually expand across campus.

The Embedded Librarian Model

This phrase has been used to describe various ways that librarians provide and maintain a presence in regard to information literacy, from adding an e-mail address to a course in a learning management system to co-teaching a class. It is best defined by Kvenild and Calkins (2011) in their edited book *Embedded Librarians:*

> Embedded librarians work closely over extended periods
> of time with non-librarian groups, whether by joining a
> semester-long course, maintaining an ongoing presence in
> online courses, participating in broad curriculum planning
> efforts, or joining the staffs of academic departments, clinical settings or performing groups. (vii)

The "common thread," according to Shumaker (2011), "is that information literacy instruction is delivered within the context of the course" (20). In this way, embedded librarianship does not differ in the spirit of the one-shot class described throughout this book, where context is always critical. In the embedded model, it is possible to have a series of one-shot sessions with a particular course or a hybrid of instructional delivery methods. If you have a good collaboration with a course instructor and an identified need for more than just a one-shot session, consider this model.

In some ways the embedded model can be more appealing to individual teaching librarians, since it is more feasible to offer successful isolated embedded librarian efforts than to initiate a campus-wide program. But like the curriculum-integrated model, it requires support from stakeholders at all levels and a "long-term strategy that addresses the needs of a user base" (Brower 2011, 3). Scalability quickly becomes a challenge with embedded librarianship. As with all information literacy efforts, librarians should be strategic. Go back to the beginning of this chapter—you are just one person. You can't be an embedded librarian for every course on campus. You will also have to sacrifice teaching as many one-shot sessions if you choose this method. Avoid overcommitment. Start with one course that you already work with, preferably one that has high expectations for information literacy skills (for example, a history research methods class) and provide two or three shots instead of just one class; you can build from there.

This book has encouraged you to remember that you are not solely responsible for students' information literacy, especially when you only have one shot with a group of students. The same attitude applies to both of these models. Seamans (2012) points out that librarians are going to have to let go of some control: "Should a faculty member embrace the information literacy concepts and take ownership of them, we must ultimately be willing to take a secondary role in how these skills are taught to students" (227–28).

Final Thoughts

You are reading this book, presumably because you teach or want to teach information literacy. You are probably already part of some sort of information literacy program. Seymour (2012) identified three general levels of information literacy integration in her interviews with librarians in West Virginia and Colorado. Your library might offer instruction at two or three of these levels.

- "Low integration": the generic library orientation, "drop-in workshops," and "online tutorials and videos" (Seymour 2012, 59).
- "Medium integration": one-shots by request, designed around course needs; online research guides for specific courses or subject areas; and "information literacy components integrated into discipline-specific courses" (59).
- "High integration": the embedded model, where the librarian has a co-teaching role and "attends several or most class meetings in a particular for-credit course" (59).

Regardless of the level of integration, in order to be a "program," your instruction efforts need to be closely tied to the curriculum of your institution and involve an intentional offering of instruction to specific classes that are identified by the librarians, faculty, and often administrators. In addition to administrative support and buy-in, other elements are necessary for a successful program, including "appropriate levels of support and training" for librarians and making sure that there is more than one librarian responsible for the library's information literacy program (Seamans 2012, 227).

The one-shot sessions you are doing now are not a waste of time. You are building solid partnerships with faculty, designing classes that are focused on student learning, and thinking about how you can be a better teacher. All of these are important elements in any information literacy program. If you are not in a position to change your library's program, keep your focus on doing your job well. Each one-shot is a seed for your growing program.

BIBLIOGRAPHY

Albrecht, Rebecca, and Sara Baron. 2002. "The Politics of Pedagogy: Expectations and Reality for Information Literacy in Librarianship." *Journal of Library Administration* 36, no. 1/2: 71–96.

American Association of School Librarians. 2007. *Standards for the 21st Century Learner.* Chicago: American Association of School Librarians. www.ala.org/aasl/sites/ala.org.aasl/files/content/guidelines andstandards/learningstandards/AASL_LearningStandards.pdf.

Anderson, Lorin W., David R. Krathwohl, and Benjamin Samuel Bloom. 2001. *A Taxonomy for Learning, Teaching, and Assessing: A Revision of Bloom's Taxonomy of Educational Objectives.* New York: Longman.

Angelo, Thomas A., and K. Patricia Cross. 1993. *Classroom Assessment Techniques: A Handbook for College Teachers.* San Francisco: Jossey-Bass.

Armstrong, Annie. 2012. "Marketing the Library's Instructional Services to Teaching Faculty: Learning from Teaching Faculty Interviews." In *College Libraries and Student Culture: What We Now Know,* edited by Lynda M. Duke and Andrew D. Asher, 31–48. Chicago: American Library Association.

Aronson, Elliot. 1978. *The Jigsaw Classroom*. Beverly Hills: Sage.

Association of College and Research Libraries. 2000. *Information Literacy Competency Standards for Higher Education*. Chicago: Association of College and Research Libraries. www.ala.org/acrl/sites/ala .org.acrl/files/content/standards/standards.pdf.

———. 2012. *Characteristics of Programs of Information Literacy that Illustrate Best Practices: A Guideline*. Chicago: Association of College and Research Libraries. www.ala.org/acrl/standards/ characteristics.

Bain, Ken. 2004. *What the Best College Teachers Do*. Cambridge, MA: Harvard University Press.

Bean, John C. 2001. *Engaging Ideas: The Professor's Guide to Integrating Writing, Critical Thinking, and Active Learning in the Classroom*. San Francisco: Jossey-Bass.

Beichner, Robert. 2008. "*The SCALE-UP Project: A Student-Centered, Active Learning Environment for Undergraduate Programs*" (invited white paper for the National Academy of Sciences, September 2008). http://sites.nationalacademies.org/dbasse/bose/ dbasse_071087.

Bergmann, Jonathan, and Aaron Sams. 2012. *Flip Your Classroom: Reach Every Student in Every Class Every Day*. Eugene, OR: International Society for Technology in Education.

Bloom, Benjamin S. 1956. *Taxonomy of Educational Objectives: The Classification of Educational Goals*. New York: Longmans, Green.

Bodi, Sonia. 2002. "How Do We Bridge the Gap Between What We Teach and What They Do? Some Thoughts on the Place of Questions in the Process of Research." *Journal of Academic Librarianship* 28, no. 3: 109–14.

Booth, Char. 2011. *Reflective Teaching, Effective Learning: Instructional Literacy for Library Educators*. Chicago: American Library Association.

Bowman, Sharon L. 2005. *The Ten-Minute Trainer: 150 Ways to Teach It Quick and Make It Stick*. San Francisco: Pfeiffer.

Brower, Matthew. 2011. "A Recent History of Embedded Librarianship: Collaboration and Partnership Building with Academics in

Learning and Research Environments." In *Embedded Librarians: Moving Beyond One-Shot Instruction,* edited by Cassandra Kvenild and Kaijsa Calkins. Chicago: Association of College and Research Libraries.

Brown, Jennifer Diane, and Thomas Scott Duke. 2006. "Librarian and Faculty Collaborative Instruction: A Phenomenological Self-Study." *Research Strategies* 20, no. 3: 171–90.

Bruff, Derek. 2009. *Teaching with Classroom Response Systems: Creating Active Learning Environments.* San Francisco: Jossey-Bass.

Choinski, Elizabeth, and Michelle Emanuel. 2006. "The One-Minute Paper and the One-Hour Class: Outcomes Assessment for One-Shot Library Instruction." *Reference Services Review* 34, no. 1: 148–55.

Clyde, Laurel A. 2005. "Librarians and Breaking Barriers to Information Literacy: Implications for Continuing Professional Development and Workplace Learning." *Library Review* 54, no. 7: 425–34.

Cole, Charles, Lynn Kennedy, and Susan Carter. 1996. "The Optimization of Online Searches Through the Labeling of a Dynamic, Situation-Dependent Information Need: The Reference Interview and Online Searching for Undergraduates Doing a Social-Science Assignment." *Information Processing & Management* 32, no. 6: 709–17.

Collins, John William, and Nancy P. O'Brien. 2003. *The Greenwood Dictionary of Education.* Westport, CT: Greenwood.

Cousin, Glynis. 2006. "An Introduction to Threshold Concepts." *Planet* 17: 4–5. www.heacademy.ac.uk/assets/documents/ subjects/gees/Planet_special_issue_fullcopy17.pdf.

Diller, Karen R., and Sue F. Phelps. 2008. "Learning Outcomes, Portfolios, and Rubrics, Oh My! Authentic Assessment of an Information Literacy Program." *Portal: Libraries and the Academy* 8, no. 1: 75–89.

Drury, Francis K. W. 1930. *Book Selection.* Chicago: American Library Association.

Duke, Lynda M., and Andrew D. Asher, eds. 2012. *College Libraries and Student Culture: What We Now Know.* Chicago: American Library Association.

English, Fenwick. 2006. "Curriculum Mapping." In *Encyclopedia of Educational Leadership and Administration*, edited by Fenwick English. Thousand Oaks: Sage.

Feldman, Devin, and Susan Sciammarella. 2000. "Both Sides of the Looking Glass: Librarian and Teaching Faculty Perceptions of Librarianship at Six Community Colleges." *College & Research Libraries* 61, no. 6: 491–98.

Filene, Peter G. 2005. *The Joy of Teaching: A Practical Guide for New College Instructors*. Chapel Hill: University of North Carolina Press.

Finkelstein, Jonathan. 2006. *Learning in Real Time: Synchronous Teaching and Learning Online*. San Francisco: Jossey-Bass.

Gasper, Deborah B., and Pamela S. Presser. 2010. "Vampires, Philosophers, and Graphic Novels: Assessing Thematic Writing Courses in the Big Read." In *Collaborative Information Literacy Assessments*, ed. Thomas Mackey and Trudi Jacobson, 155–74. New York: Neal-Schuman.

Gilchrist, Debra, and Anne Zald. 2008. "Instruction and Program Design Through Assessment." In *Information Literacy Instruction Handbook*, edited by Christopher N. Cox and Elizabeth Blakesley Lindsay, 164–92. Chicago: Association of College and Research Libraries.

Hattie, John. 2009. *Visible Learning: A Synthesis of Over 800 Meta-Analyses Relating to Achievement*. London: Routledge.

Head, Allison, and Michael Eisenberg. 2009. "Lessons Learned: How College Students Seek Information in the Digital Age." In *Project Information Literacy: First Year Report with Student Survey Findings*. University of Washington. http://projectinfolit.org/publications/.

Hofer, Amy R., Lori Townsend, and Korey Brunetti. 2012. "Troublesome Concepts and Information Literacy: Investigating Threshold Concepts for IL Instruction." *Portal: Libraries and the Academy* 12, no. 4: 387–405.

Jeffries, Shellie. 2000. "The Librarian as Networker: Setting the Standard for Higher Education." In *The Collaborative Imperative: Librarians and Faculty Working Together in the Information Universe*, edited by Richard Raspa and Dane Ward, 114–29. Chicago: Association of College and Research Libraries.

Johnson, David W., and Roger T. Johnson. 1999. *Learning Together and Alone: Cooperative, Competitive, and Individualistic Learning.* 5th ed. Boston: Allyn and Bacon.

Kennedy, Lynn, Charles Cole, and Susan Carter. 1999. "The False Focus in Online Searching: The Particular Case of Undergraduates Seeking Information for Course Assignments in the Humanities and Social Sciences." *Reference & User Services Quarterly* 38, no. 3: 267–73.

Ko, Susan Schor, and Steve Rossen. 2010. *Teaching Online: A Practical Guide.* 3rd ed. New York: Routledge.

Kuhlthau, Carol Collier. 1991. "Inside the Search Process: Information Seeking from the User's Perspective." *Journal of the American Society for Information Science* 42, no. 5: 361–71.

———. 1994. "Students and the Information Search Process: Zones of Intervention for Librarians." *Advances in Librarianship* 18: 57–72.

———. 2004. *Seeking Meaning: A Process Approach to Library and Information Services.* Westport, CT: Libraries Unlimited.

Kuhlthau, Carol C., Jannica Heinström, and Ross J. Todd. 2008. "The 'Information Search Process' Revisited: Is the Model Still Useful?" *Information Research* 13, no. 4: 45.

Kvenild, Cassandra, and Kaijsa Calkins. 2011. "Introduction." In *Embedded Librarians: Moving Beyond One-Shot Instruction,* edited by Cassandra Kvenild and Kaijsa Calkins. Chicago: Association of College and Research Libraries.

Long, Casey, and Milind Shrikhande. 2010. "Using Citation Analysis to Evaluate and Improve Information Literacy Instruction." In *Collaborative Information Literacy Assessments,* edited by Thomas Mackey and Trudi Jacobson, 5–24. New York: Neal-Schuman.

Lyman, Frank T. 1981. "The Responsive Classroom Discussion: The Inclusion of All Students." In *Mainstreaming Digest,* edited by Audrey Anderson, 109–13. College Park: University of Maryland Press.

McKnight, Michelynn. 2010. *The Agile Librarian's Guide to Thriving in Any Institution*. Santa Barbara, CA: Libraries Unlimited.

Meulemans, Yvonne N., and Allison Carr. 2013. "Not at Your Service: Building Genuine Faculty-Librarian Partnerships." *Reference Services Review* 41, no. 1: 80–90.

Meyer, Jan, and Ray Land. 2006. *Overcoming Barriers to Student Understanding: Threshold Concepts and Troublesome Knowledge*. London: Routledge.

Millis, Barbara J., and Philip G. Cottell. 1998. *Cooperative Learning for Higher Education Faculty*. American Council on Education, Oryx Press Series on Higher Education. Rowan and Littlefield.

Morgan, Norah, and Juliana Saxton. 2006. *Asking Better Questions*. 2nd ed. Markham, ON: Pembroke.

Nilson, Linda B. 2010. *Teaching at Its Best: A Research-Based Resource for College Instructors*. 3rd ed. San Francisco: Jossey-Bass.

Nutefall, Jennifer E., and Phyllis Mentzell Ryder. 2010. "The Timing of the Research Question: First-Year Writing Faculty and Instruction Librarians' Differing Perspectives." *Portal: Libraries and the Academy* 10, no. 4: 437–49.

Oakleaf, Megan, and Steven Hoover, Beth Woodard, Jennifer Corbin, Randy Hensley, Diana Wakimoto, Christopher Hollister, et al. 2012. "Notes from the Field." *Communications in Information Literacy* 6, no. 1: 5–23.

Popham, W. James 2010. *Everything School Leaders Need to Know About Assessment*. Thousand Oaks, CA: Corwin.

Radcliff, Carolyn, Mary Jensen, Julie Salem, Kenneth Burhanna, and Joseph Gedeon. 2007. *A Practical Guide to Information Literacy Assessment for Academic Librarians*. Westport, CT: Libraries Unlimited.

Raspa, Richard, and Dane Ward. 2000. *The Collaborative Imperative: Librarians and Faculty Working Together in the Information Universe*. Chicago: Association of College and Research Libraries.

Reeves, Linda, Judy McMillan, and Renata Gibson. 2008. "Keep Them Engaged: Cooperative Learning with the Jigsaw Method." *In*

Practical Pedagogy for Library Instructors: 17 Innovative Strategies to Improve Student Learning, edited by Douglas Cook and Ryan Sittler, 77–86. Chicago: Association of College and Research Libraries.

Rockman, Ilene F. 2004. *Integrating Information Literacy into the Higher Education Curriculum: Practical Models for Transformation.* San Francisco: Jossey-Bass.

Saunders, Laura. 2007. "Regional Accreditation Organizations' Treatment of Information Literacy: Definitions, Collaboration, and Assessment." *Journal of Academic Librarianship* 33, no. 3: 317–26.

Scherdin, Mary Jane. 1994. *Discovering Librarians: Profiles of a Profession.* Chicago: Association of College and Research Libraries.

Seamans, Nancy H. 2012. "Information Literacy Reality Check." In *Transforming Information Literacy Programs: Intersecting Frontiers of Self, Library Culture, and Campus Community,* edited by Carroll Wetzel Wilkinson and Courtney Bruch, 45–71. Chicago: Association of College and Research Libraries.

Seymour, Celene. 2012. "Ethnographic Study of Information Literacy Librarians' Work Experience: A Report from Two States." In *Transforming Information Literacy Programs: Intersecting Frontiers of Self, Library Culture, and Campus Community,* edited by Carroll Wetzel Wilkinson and Courtney Bruch, 45–71. Chicago: Association of College and Research Libraries.

Shumaker, David. 2011. "Beyond Instruction: Creating New Roles for Embedded Librarians." In *Embedded Librarians: Moving Beyond One-Shot Instruction,* edited by Cassandra Kvenild and Kaijsa Calkins. Chicago: Association of College and Research Libraries.

Smilkstein, Rita. 2006. "Constructivism." In *The Praeger Handbook of Learning and the Brain,* edited by Sheryl Feinstein, 154–57. Westport, CT: Praeger.

Smith, Karl A. 2000. "Going Deeper: Formal Small-Group Learning in Large Classes." *New Directions for Teaching & Learning* 81: 25.

Stevens, R. J. 2008. "Cooperative Learning." In *Encyclopedia of Educational Psychology,* edited by Neil J. Salkind and Kristin Rasmussen, vol. 1, 187–93. Thousand Oaks, CA: Sage.

Taba, Hilda. 1962. *Curriculum Development: Theory and Practice.* New York: Harcourt, Brace and World.

Townsend, Lori, Korey Brunetti, and Amy R. Hofer. 2011. "Threshold Concepts and Information Literacy." *Portal: Libraries and the Academy* 11, no. 3: 853–69.

U.S. Department of Education, National Center for Education Statistics. 2012. Supplemental Academic Libraries Survey (ALS) 2010 Tables to NCES 2012–365. http://nces.ed.gov/pubs2012/2012365_1.pdf.

Veldof, Jerilyn R. 2006. *Creating the One-Shot Library Workshop: A Step-by-Step Guide* Chicago: American Library Association.

Wallace, Susan. 2009. *A Dictionary of Education.* New York: Oxford University Press.

Walter, Scott. 2005. "Improving Instruction: What Librarians Can Learn from the Study of College Teaching." In *Currents and Convergence: Navigating the Rivers of Change, Proceedings of the Twelfth National Conference of the Association of College and Research Libraries, April 7–10, 2005*, Minneapolis, Minnesota, edited by Hugh A. Thompson, 1–17. Chicago: Association of College and Research Libraries. http://kuscholarworks.ku.edu/dspace/handle/1808/262.

Ward, Dane. 1997. "How Is Information Literacy Different from Bibliographic Instruction?" *LOEX News* 24, no. 4 (Winter 1997): 9.

Wilkinson, Carroll Wetzel, and Courtney Bruch, eds. 2012. *Transforming Information Literacy Programs: Intersecting Frontiers of Self, Library Culture, and Campus Community.* Chicago: Association of College and Research Libraries.

Zald, Anne E., and Michelle Millet. 2012. "Hitching Your Wagon to Institutional Goals." In *Transforming Information Literacy Programs: Intersecting Frontiers of Self, Library Culture, and Campus Community,* edited by Caroll Wetzel Wilkinson and Courtney Bruch, 119–30. Chicago: Association of College and Research Libraries.

INDEX

f denotes figures; *t* denotes tables